# THE ART OF
# COACHING
*for*
# SERVANT
# LEADERSHIP

## A Guide for Coaches, Managers, and Anyone Who Wants to Bring Out the BEST in Others

# Ann McGee-Cooper
# & Deborah Welch
## with Duane Trammell

ANN MCGEE-COOPER AND ASSOCIATES, INC.
Dallas

Cover and Text Design by Suzanne Pustejovsky Design, Austin, Texas
Composition by Timm Chamberlain, Dallas, Texas

ISBN 978-1517493851

# DEDICATION

"Awareness is not a giver of solace—it is just the opposite. It is a disturber and an awakener. Able leaders are usually sharply awake and reasonably disturbed. They are not seekers after solace. They have their own inner serenity."

—*Robert K. Greenleaf*

We three want to dedicate this book to honor all of you who have honored us with your trust and welcomed us as a coach into your innermost life challenges. We are especially blessed to have learned from you the mutuality of the role as coach. For unless we are also on a journey of learning and growing, how can we possibly bring value and insight to others? The most valuable insights often come at the conclusion of each coaching session when we ask, "What brought the most value during this time together and are there ways we can improve our support for you?" What we have learned in the pattern of responses has surprised us and stretched our own growth in unprecedented ways.

We also often risk sharing our own lives and challenges with you. As these dialogues become two-way, we learn to be curious together, listen for Spirit, and prepare ourselves for each meeting or call by moving our ego out of the way. Then something amazing begins to speak through us. It is the courage, candor, and deep wisdom coming through each of you that awakens something deep within us in ways we could never have imagined. The act and art of servant leadership is learning to surrender in humility and listen for what wants to be heard and come through. We know that we could not have grown and learned so much without the deep wisdom reflected back and offered candidly by each of those special persons who honored us with this deep mutual learning time together.

We especially want to thank Ginny Gilmore, who has been a pioneer devoted to mutual learning in partnership. Mature servant leadership requires that we do much more than read books or learn skills but that we grow toward greater self-actualization and toward our best possible selves. Ginny, whether you are partnering on a coaching call, co-designing or co-facilitating a servant leadership circle session, dialoguing with us on a principle we are writing about, or trailblazing within your community, you are always devoted to compassion in every relationship and taking risks in order to "be the change" for a more caring community that you are bringing into the world. Sophia Foundation is an exemplary model for servant leadership in communities.

To all who have worked with us in servant leadership coaching, from the young children who were our wise, "old soul" students, to all the many adults who opened your lives to share in respectful searching, we give heartfelt thanks and hope you find our writing reflecting the full measure of what you helped us discover. It is our greatest hope that we will have added to the work of Robert K. Greenleaf in bringing his insights into the unfolding relationship of self-awareness and personal transformation.

> "...the servant views any problem in the world
> as *in here*, not *out there*. And if a flaw in the
> world is to be remedied, to the servant the
> process of change starts *in here*, not *out there*."
>
> —*Robert K. Greenleaf*

# CONTENTS

# FOREWORD
## by
## Helen Burt

FOR MANY YEARS, I HAVE
had a large note card displayed
in my office with one sentence
that is as haunting as it is
inspiring. It reads:

*"If you're not scaring yourself, you're probably
not reaching your full potential."*

The person who handed that
card to me—back in 1987—
was Ann McGee-Cooper. She
had been brought in by my
employer at the time, Texas
Utilities, to help us think
creatively about how to lift
performance, both for ourselves
and our teams.

The reason that sentence resonates for me is because of what it says about servant leadership. On one level, the idea of "scaring yourself" means having the courage to take your own risks. But if you want a team full of people who are also willing to "scare themselves" in order to reach their full potential, they need to know their leader will support and guide them.

This has been a tenet of leadership that I have carried with me throughout my career, and the seed was planted all those years ago by Ann. Of course, seeds of wisdom need watering and tending, which is why Ann's continued coaching has been so necessary for me. It has kept the seeds of servant leadership, which I learned early in my career, alive and growing in new and sometimes unexpected ways.

In one of my first coaching sessions with Ann, she told me and my team about the *Herrmann Brain Dominance Instrument*, or HBDI®, a tool that helps identify the thinking preferences we demonstrate in making decisions. What an amazing process of self-discovery this was for me! I learned that I am very focused on the future and full of ideas and creative thinking. Yet, there is a flip side. I also learned that not all my ideas are good and I tend to completely overlook the necessary steps in achieving the vision.

The most important takeaway, however, was the process itself. By understanding and acknowledging my own gifts and shortcomings with my teammates, they feel more comfortable doing the same. I give voice to those who may be intimidated by title (or the sheer force of my personality). I learn invaluable things about each person on my team, and they learn that I absolutely depend on them to help us succeed.

Since those first interactions with Ann and her business Partner, Duane Trammell, I have continued to grow in my own leadership, learning to coach others in the practice of servant leadership. In particular, I am drawn to coaching through storytelling, one of the many tools and techniques explored in this excellent book.

One story that I like to tell is an experience of being led by a true servant-leader. I was working in a company in crisis, and a new CEO had been brought in to "right the ship." As a member of the senior leadership team, I assumed a change at the top would mean the end of my shelf life. New leaders almost always clean house.

So when the CEO called the senior team into a meeting on day two, we were filled with dread. We all dressed in black for the occasion. For the first 15 minutes, our new leader delivered what was probably a wonderful speech, but no one in the room was listening. No one was breathing.

Finally, he stopped, put his tablet and pen down, and looked at each of us. "I am sensing I need to say something to you," he said. Here we go, I thought. Then he said the four most powerful words I have ever heard from a leader: "You will not fail." Everyone let out a sigh of relief. "It is my job to support you and make sure I do everything possible to help you succeed," he added. With that, we took out our pens and notebooks, started asking questions, and were all suddenly committed to support this person we had just met.

I tell this story because it speaks to how important it is for leaders to reaffirm their commitment to the team and the individual. It reminds us of the awe-inspiring responsibility—and privilege—we have to help our teams overcome their fears and invite them to reach their full potential.

Many more stories and lessons like this are contained in the pages that follow. I know that you will come away with greater self-awareness and confidence as a servant-leader and coach. You will learn how Deborah Welch, the lead writer and very gifted servant-leader coach, proposed the idea for this book to Ann and how Duane Trammell, co-founder of Ann McGee-Cooper & Associates, and others collaborated in the process.

I am grateful to Ann for her many years of wonderful coaching and the profound impact she has had on my life and career, and I wish all of you the best on your journey.

**Helen Burt**
**Senior Vice President, Corporate Affairs**
**PG&E Corporation**

# THE AUTHORS

## Ann McGee-Cooper, Ed.D.

 is a business futurist, owns her own consulting company, and has worked with organizations for four decades in innovation, the politics of change, and servant leadership. She holds degrees from the University of Texas, Southern Methodist University, and a doctorate from Columbia University. Ann has worked in an unusually wide variety of workplaces—including coal mines of West Virginia, corporate boardrooms of international engineering and construction companies, the Culture Committee of Southwest Airlines, a NASCAR race team, and governmental agencies.

For her international work in servant leadership, Ann has been honored with two honorary doctorates from Trinity Western University and Sterling College. She also received the Good Neighbor Award from Southwest Airlines and was recognized by the International Professional Women's Alliance for pace-setting work in mentoring and servant leadership.

## Deborah Welch, Ph.D.

 coaches entrepreneurs and leaders in foundations, school districts, colleges, and corporations. Her studies of collaborative intelligence and of the very best of what is possible in leadership in organizations led her in 2008 to co-create, along with Ann McGee-Cooper and Virginia Gilmore, the first Virtual Servant Leadership Learning Community (VSLLC®). VSLLC® is a six-month program in which dedicated servant-leaders from around the world and across a variety of industries enhance their capacity to grow as servant-leaders and create connections for greater support in the work of servant leadership. In addition to serving in corporate and community e-learning and leadership coaching at AMCA, Deborah is also an award-winning faculty member at Capella University. She teaches The Psychology of Leadership and guides dissertation research in the area of self-awareness and leadership.

Deborah has published several articles. Most recently she co-wrote, "Strengths Based Leadership Coaching" with a research team, which has been published in Consulting Psychology Journal. She brings a wide array of tools and processes into her coaching work based on several decades of experience. She is known for coaching that helps leaders achieve results and grow into their best selves.

## Duane Trammell, M.Ed.

 is founding Partner, President and COO of Ann McGee-Cooper and Associates, Inc. and has been collaborating with Ann for thirty-three years.

Duane enjoys writing, researching, and developing materials in servant leadership. He has co-authored *Time Management for Unmanageable People, You Don't Have To Go Home from Work Exhausted!, Being the Change: Profiles from Our Servant Leadership Learning Community*, and a second edition of *Awakening Your Sleeping Genius: A Journaling Approach to Personal Growth and Servant Leadership*. Trammell participated in Ann McGee-Cooper's early research on genius/giftedness and combined it with Robert Greenleaf's concepts on servant leadership to produce the journal.

As a business educator and leadership development specialist, Duane's specialty is writing and delivering participant-based learning. Educational awards have included "Dallas Teacher of the Year" and being named as "One of Three Outstanding Teachers in Texas."

# INTRODUCTION

WE ARE ENTHUSED TO offer this book of principles and stories on servant leadership coaching. You will find stories illustrating how growing as a servant-leader can be a liberating experience resulting in engagement, energy, meaning at work, and enhanced capacities to achieve business results. This is in great contrast with what is happening in many organizations today where so many leaders find themselves weighed down with increasingly tough economic and political issues. Facing unprecedented challenges, they can become cynical and disempowered. Yet at the same time, something remarkable is happening for a small but growing number of leaders who are thriving, contributing powerfully in the workplace, and growing into their best selves as leaders. Many of these individuals identify themselves as servant-leaders. And even if they don't use the word *servant-leader*, they are meeting what Robert Greenleaf calls the "best test" of servant leadership. The test is that those they work with are growing wiser, freer, stronger, and are more likely themselves to care for and serve others. Not only is this way of leading powerful for impacting Customer* satisfaction, Partner satisfaction, and profitability, it is the very foundation of the kind of legacy many of us want to leave for our children and grandchildren and future generations in the workplace.

> *The difference manifests itself in the care taken–first to make sure that the other people's highest priority needs are being served. The best test, and difficult to administer, is this: "Do those served grow as persons? Do they, while being served, become healthier, wiser, freer, more autonomous and more likely to serve others?"* [1]

When a culture based in servant leadership develops, we can see the emergence of the same characteristics that are evident in the "Best Companies to Work For" listed in *Fortune Magazine* or at Forbes.com. Companies like Starbucks, Southwest Airlines, and TDIndustries consistently demonstrate that organizations can reach extraordinary levels of performance and trust when a servant leadership culture develops. Individuals and organizations such as these experience empowerment at all levels and become strongly engaged at work. It doesn't happen perfectly for

---

*Note: We have taken a convention first learned from Colleen Barrett, President Emeritus of Southwest Airlines, to capitalize words such as Client, Customer, Company, Employee, and Partner to show respect. It costs nothing yet communicates a special relationship.

every person all the time, but when the fabric of the organizational culture develops steadily over time there are remarkable results and high levels of engagement and enjoyment at work.

A growing number of great books and research articles make the case for why servant leadership is a powerful approach.[2] What is not so apparent, however, is how leaders grow to become greater servant-leaders. To lead by serving seems highly idealistic and impractical in a world where so many of our systems are dysfunctional and gridlocked and where destructive or unethical behaviors happen within the organization. Servant-leaders follow their chosen path in spite of profoundly difficult organizational challenges, drawing deeply on their convictions and values to bring exceptional performance along with a high level of ethics and human spirit back to our organizations and communities.

In this book, you will read stories exemplifying how that happens for leaders at every level of experience and responsibility in organizations, communities, and families. You will understand the key role that coaching plays in drawing out the unique, inherent qualities that make servant-leaders strong. And you will learn essential principles for coaching relationships. We have found that the most powerful way to grow as a servant-leader is to build true *coaching* relationships.

## Coaching for Servant Leadership

The word *coach* actually originated from the idea of a stagecoach in the early days of transportation. A coach is a vehicle that transports people from one place to another, much like a person who is a good coach and travels beside you, creating a relationship that is a powerful alliance. This is different from coaching that provides advice or instruction on the "right" way to accomplish something (according to them). Advice can be helpful if you want to learn how to work a computer, but the work of servant leadership is about growing as a person. A servant-leader coach offers no simple answers; profound transformation requires changing old habits, searching deeply within ourselves, and learning how to cooperate with the process of growth. An intimate servant leadership coaching relationship challenges both coach and leader to work well even in difficult situations of internal conflict where we sometimes stand in the way of our own possibilities.

The mission of this book is to inspire and support leaders who want to develop greater coaching capacities. Servant leadership coaching is a discovery process. Coaches learn to grow themselves and others in ways that facilitate high-trust relationships, stronger accountability, and more energy and meaning for the leader.

## Stories Tell the Story

Throughout this book we will highlight stories of real-life servant-leader coaches and their struggles and subsequent learning. Stories are important in coaching for a variety of reasons. Stories can speak to us on many levels, provoke imagination, and open our servants' hearts. There are, however, different learning styles among readers. If you read the stories and want more action ideas, look for the "Reflections" at the end of the chapters or try using the chart "Coaching with a Servant's Heart" in appendix A as a focus point for practices to experiment with as you read.

## Growing as a Servant-Leader

Before delving into coaching, we want to provide an example of servant leadership within an organization. In this first story Howard Behar, former president of Starbucks North America, sheds light on the kind of inner growth that servant leadership requires. Howard Behar partnered closely with chairman and president Howard Schultz during the period when Starbucks grew from a little Seattle company to 15,000 stores in forty-seven countries around the world. In the first few years, they were working on visioning who they wanted to be and setting some big goals for the organization. Howard describes how they worked to set BHAGs (big hairy audacious goals). These are goals that go beyond numbers, like "We want to have 2,000 stores," to a goal that *attaches to your soul, something that when you get up every day you just cannot let go of.* With involvement from baristas, store managers, officers, directors, and Customers, the words used to describe the Starbucks vision was that it will be *"one of the most well-known and respected organizations in the world, and we will be known for nurturing and inspiring the human spirit."* With that in mind, Howard began to ask himself every day, "How can I inspire human spirit today?"[3]

Inspiring human spirit has a deep meaning for Howard. At a conference on servant leadership, he shared a personal story which illustrates the challenges he faced when working as an officer of a public company prior to coming to Starbucks and the way he committed to his own growth in the midst of the struggle. Just a few weeks after being recruited for his strengths, Howard was called in by the chairman of the board, Walker, who said, "Howard, I want to give you a little advice now that you are going to be an executive. . . . One of the things that I have noticed about you, Howard, is that you always wear your heart on your sleeve. Everybody always knows how you are feeling and what you are thinking about. A good executive will hold his cards a little closer to his vest. Do not always let everybody know what you are thinking about. When you go to meetings and you are excited about something, your passion just comes right through. A good executive might hold a little bit of that back."

> "Our success is directly related to our clarity and honesty about who we are and who we're not."

So at twenty-seven years old, Howard was asking himself how he could change *himself.* He began writing little reminders on slips of paper to show less passion. After several months he said to his wife Lyn, "I regret the day that I ever took that promotion. I was loving what I was doing. I was contributing. I was feeling good about myself. I loved being a part of everything. I could be who I was. Now I hate this work and want to quit." Being very supportive, his wife said, "Okay, do what you need to do, but why not go talk to somebody first?" When Howard talked with his coworkers, he found that they were not happy with the way he had been trying to change. They said, "We wanted you to be an officer of the Company because of what you brought to the rest of us—passion and creativity and inviting the rest of us to speak our minds. Now you aren't giving us what we thought we were going to get."

Ultimately, Howard stepped back and asked himself some important questions. He adds, "Our success is directly related to our clarity and honesty about who we are and who we're not." The chairman's words had a negative effect on Howard—an effect we can have on others without even realizing it. Howard invites all of us to listen to what we are saying to our kids or to our co-workers, observing, "Sometimes we just want to project ourselves on other people instead of listening to them and recognizing who they are." This was a time that he made a choice to stop and reflect. "Like most of us I was just living my life. I never really sat down and said, 'What do I stand for?' So my journey began on that day and I started writing things down. 'What are my values? What do I stand for? When I say *honesty* what does that mean? What do I want to leave behind? How do I want to treat my family? What matters to me?'"

This is one of many stories Howard tells illustrating how he has stayed true to the mission to inspire human spirit. He learned that honest inquiry and reflection was at the core of inspiring the servant-leader journey. In contrast, the culture in most organizations asks us to spend all our hours performing and tolerates little or no time for in-depth inquiry. Howard made the choice to bring himself, his passion, and his unique gifts into the organization, and his presence inspired others. His example exemplifies the kind of growth and potential we work toward with servant leadership coaching.

Ann shares how her own growth was supercharged when Robert Greenleaf himself acted as her servant-leader coach and invited her to look within.

| Ann McGee-Cooper
## The Spirit of Servant Leadership Coaching

When I reflect on the time that I was coached by Robert Greenleaf, I remember thinking of him as a guru. I wanted Greenleaf to give me advice about a specific program I was developing and how I could be a messenger of his vision of servant leadership. I wanted him to tell me the answers. That was not at all the spirit of Greenleaf's understanding of servant leadership or his role in it. What he did instead was be very attentive to me. He seemed fascinated by *my* ideas.

Greenleaf used active listening, mirroring back what I would say in a different way. It wasn't just his vocabulary—it was the tone of voice and how he processed what I said before he mirrored back. He wasn't embellishing my words; he helped me hear myself at a different level. I remember how he listened in a different, very quiet way. He listened at a deep level. He helped me to honor my deepest self by using a lot of silence. When a person allows spaces of silence in a conversation, you begin hearing yourself in a different way.

The way he mirrored back to me was vital to my heart. He connected me to many thoughts and thought leaders but always emphasized, "Ann, listen to your spirit. You already know all of the answers to the questions you're asking. By creating more space in your life and reverence for that inner wisdom, you'll find it. As Thomas Keating says, 'Silence is God's first language; everything else is a poor translation.'"

| Deborah Welch

## Ways to Benefit from This Approach to Servant Leadership

If you, like Ann, were able to sit in a chair next to Robert Greenleaf, what would that experience be like? Has there been a time you have been heard deeply? Although every coach offers a unique style of coaching, the stories, ideas, and practices we will share are based on a depth of listening that Greenleaf modeled and that is unusual in our frenetic work environments. In this book, we will explore more about servant leadership listening and other essential elements of servant leadership coaching. Here are a few thoughts on how to experience the greatest benefit.

### Believe you are a leader

If you are wondering how much the word *leader* fits you, we are not referring to just the formally designated leader or the C-suite executives. We also mean coaches, teachers, family members, community figures, and organizational team members. We all have some level of influence on others, so we all have opportunities to lead. These ideas can apply in a variety of settings. In fact, many people find that change that affects their families impacts them first, and later it influences the way they lead in an organization. Conversely, the learning you experience leading as a servant in the organization can apply to how you relate in your family.

**Integrate the material**
Since servant leadership coaching is relational at its core, think about inviting a learning partner on the journey. Preferably, this should be someone who listens deeply and helps you live into your best self. Discuss the ideas and stories in this book with that person as you encounter them. You can immediately begin applying the principles of servant leadership coaching with each other.

Another idea: As you read the principles and essential insights presented in this book, experiment with applying one each week.

**For professional coaches**
This is not intended as a comprehensive guide to coaching, but it can enhance your coaching work if you consider integrating your own stories and principles and reflect on the way you aspire to coach.

**For managers, family leaders, community leaders, classroom teachers—and leaders of all kinds**
Servant leadership coaching can be practiced at multiple levels: peer to peer, supervisor to Employee, or coaching upward on the organizational chart. Teachers may coach students as well as be coached by someone younger. Friends who want to grow as servant-leaders may set up a coaching exchange to hold each other accountable to greater growth and support. Even if you don't see yourself as a coach, believe that each of us has the capacity to enhance the ways we serve others at work, in our families, and in wider community relationships.

Deborah Welch

## The Writing of this Book

If you are feeling doubtful or cynical about just how much servant leadership can apply in your organization, you are not alone. The case for why servant leadership works is clearly expressed in several books.[4] Here is a story about my own growth as a servant-leader, beginning with my own doubt and cynicism about leadership in organizations.

In the eighties I experienced an organizational takeover. The teams that I loved seemed to be dismantled almost overnight. We had had strong self-managing teams that were sharing leadership and providing services to thousands of families through a great organization. Even though all the same managers stayed in place after a new company took over, fear shot through the organization. I was told that good leaders make quicker decisions and don't spend as much time collaborating. I was deeply disheartened, and eventually that led me to go back for my doctorate to learn more about leadership and trust. When I saw what Ann and the Ann McGee-Cooper and Associates (AMCA) team were doing in organizations like Southwest Airlines and TDIndustries, I understood that the high ideals that I was reading about in leadership books could flourish in practical ways in organizations, and cultures could develop to support this emergence. In my many trips to Dallas, I learned how this approach applies in a Servant Leadership Learning Community (SLLC®) made up of individuals from corporations, police and probation workers, hospitals, schools, non-profit organizations, entrepreneurial endeavors, and more. I began working with Ann and others to create ways to share the principles for growing as a servant-leader in a learning community with others. The stories of how the ideals of servant leadership were being lived every day by individuals and whole organizations benefited me, my doctoral students, and my coaching Clients. I asked Ann to write this book with me to help others gain from what I was so blessed to discover.

This book is filled with stories, especially stories from Ann about coaching Clients in servant leadership, along with the learning that she experienced directly when working with Robert Greenleaf. I have arranged them based on the essential elements of servant leadership coaching.

In addition to Ann's and Duane's stories, we draw heavily on stories from Dawna Markova who, like Ann, is a world-renowned leadership coach working with top executives in Fortune 100 companies. Dawna has deeply inspired us with who she is and the work she does. We have read her coaching stories over and over and find that they weave together many levels of wisdom.

We will also read stories from within our Servant Leadership Learning Community, a deeply dedicated group of extraordinary leaders who provide additional perspectives and gems of insight. These contributors include **Shaunna Black, Cynthia Watson, Matt Kosec, Rebecca Braden, Jenny Inge, Ginny Gilmore, Christa Williams, Steve Parker, Cliff Watson, Maddie Watson,** and **Bob Kidwell.** Biographies of those who contributed stories are listed in appendix D at the end of this book.

Although many stories in this book are from professional coaches, some are from managers and others are from family members coaching each other. Remember, *one or more principles are embedded in every story*, and these same principles can be used in *any* partnership which has as its purpose a mutual desire to support one another's growth.

## The Structure of the Book

As we brainstormed a structure for the book that could work with the many different voices we wanted to represent, Duane provided "aha" moments that were central to how the book came together. Like the guide of a mountain climbing expedition, Duane made it possible to make the climb to complete this book.

Within the pages, different voices illustrate essential elements of servant leadership coaching. We have used flags to indicate when the voice you are reading is changing from Ann's to mine, or to Duane's, or to another servant leadership coach's voice.

The first four chapters outline the principles of servant leadership coaching and illustrate them with a variety of poignant stories. Chapter 5 offers concrete ideas and tools to apply the principles. The Conclusion collates and emphasizes takeaways from the book and shares a moving story about the power of visioning between a father and daughter.

*A Tip: Do not ignore the appendices section or you will miss valuable gold!*

- **Appendix A** contains a chart that describes the fourteen essential principles of servant leadership coaching. The chart will help you summarize the book's coaching principles and track your development in building new habits to cement servant-leader coaching practices. Using your own coaching principles and practices, you can adapt the chart to fit your experiences and stories.

- **Appendix B** describes how one servant-leader has approached his struggle to find time for leading as a servant.

- In **Appendix C**, Ann explains how she uses coaching notes and gives examples.

- **Appendix D** provides biographies of the principal contributors to the book.

# I

# LIFTING UP GREATNESS AS A SERVANT LEADER COACH

IN MOST ORGANIZATIONS too many people leave their strengths on the sidelines. Stephen Covey said it clearly:

*Surveys report that more than half of all American workers*

1

*believe they could double their productivity, yet they don't. . . . [And] the vast majority of the workforce possesses more intelligence and talents than their jobs require, or even allow them to use. . . . [If humans were like cars it would be as if] we usually have eight cylinders available to us, yet we often use only four cylinders at work.*[5]

Research on Employee engagement shows us that only one in eleven Employees in the U.S. (9 percent) report that they use their strengths at work.[6] The majority of people work at a fraction of their capacity. Their strengths, talents, and gifts are often overlooked or misused either by themselves or others. Servant leadership, in contrast, is all about the exploration and activation of people's gifts and strengths. As servant-leaders, we serve others by seeing their gifts and talents and freeing them to use them.

### In this chapter, we will explore

1. *Why coaches help their Partners discover what lights them up, and how when people are aligned with innate gifts, it re-energizes the brain*

2. *How working on our own strengths as a coach is a path to serving with humility and maturity*

3. *How reflecting on our unique gifts over the course of many experiences and years, and noticing how they connect with our life purpose, can help uncover a way to claim greater use of our genius and lead to greater contributions in the way we serve*

4. *How a servant leadership coaching initiative leads to triple-bottom-line results, including profitability*

**❝ It is vital to learn how to discover our gifts and strengths and what it is that lights us up!"**

When Dr. Dawna Markova was interviewed, she spoke about how focusing on our innate gifts is essential in coaching leaders.

## LEARNING WHAT LIGHTS YOU UP (AND WHAT LIGHTS UP YOUR COACHING PARTNER) | Dawna Markova

MY RESEARCH SHOWED ME that we are born with or at a very early age we develop particular synaptic connections that enable each of us to perceive and receive the world in a particular way. When you think in these ways, it literally re-energizes your brain. This is very important because your brain uses more energy than any other single organ in your body. It needs a huge amount of glucose, for instance, to make a decision. If you spend hours on email, for example, you will use up a lot of the glucose you have available to your whole system. If you then have to make an important decision or think through something that's really important, you'll need to re-energize your brain.

What research and experience have taught me is that when people are aligned with these innate and energizing ways of thinking, they light up and come more alive; they don't burn out. For example, one of my thinking talents is storytelling. I might be really hungry or tired or whatever, but if I start telling you stories, I wake up and can go for hours. I feel more and more energized.

You've probably noticed this lighting up in other people and attributed it to something else. Several years ago, my son and his wife did an experiment: he videotaped fifty people as she was asking each one a series of evocative questions about their lives. One woman, for example, was a personal trainer. She was smiling normally as she answered questions about her work. But when she talked about mentoring others to be trainers, her whole face lit up. We've shown that videotape to hundreds of people and everyone notices that particular moment because she begins to unconsciously shine. Her brain is literally energized by mentoring others.

The question is how do you create a relationship between those innate thinking talents and the challenges an individual is facing? These talents, by the way, are not the same thing as skills which are learned, which do not reenergize our brains. I'm very good at doing research. For instance, I had to learn to do it when I was in graduate school, but it's a skill, not a talent of mine. I have learned to hire others who have analytic talents, which frees me up to write and tell stories. In summary, what I'm saying is that it's necessary to tease out and discern what the actual ways of thinking are that energize each individual's brain and life.[7]

| Deborah Welch

## HOW ATTENDING TO UNIQUE GIFTS ENERGIZES YOUR COACHING PARTNER

Dawna's insights remind us of the importance of discerning between a skill and a talent or gift. A skill can de-energize us, so it is vital to learn how to discover our gifts and strengths and what it is that lights us up.

There are many tools and methods that can be used. The AMCA team uses the *Herrmann Brain Dominance Instrument*® to find strengths through preference.[8] Dawna and her team use software they developed called *The Smart Navigator*®.[9] *Strengthsfinder*® is another assessment developed by Gallup Organization that is very popular and used by millions.[10]

Ann and Duane have also created the book *Awakening Your Sleeping Genius: A Journaling Approach to Personal Growth and Servant Leadership*,[11] which provides a series of activities to discover gifts and uniqueness for servant-leaders. More information about tools can be found in the "Conclusion" section of this book. But first, it is worth considering that although tools are important and a beginning point to identify strengths, they can also become a short-lived exercise if a strengths philosophy does not provide a foundation to sustain us through the difficult times on the journey to discover and use our strengths. For example, chapter 3 discusses the ways strengths can be misused or overused. Also, in the middle of trying to develop your strengths, it can suddenly seem self-indulgent to focus on learning about your own strengths. Yet strengths work is a key path to serving with humility as a servant-leader coach.

In "Coaching with a Servant's Heart" in appendix A, you will find our emphasis on how doing great coaching requires that we have the courage to live to our fullest potential. Robert Greenleaf has shown how the commitment to serve requires attending to our uniqueness and to what lights us up. Greenleaf wrote about what he called *entheos*, "being lit up from within." He worked on developing this in himself. He said, "We need to cultivate strength, nurtured by entheos." Another way to look at the meaning of entheos is as a spiritedness and being "lit up from within." He added, "This is the central idea of maturity: to keep your private lamp lighted as you venture forth." In another passage, he reflects how difficult it was for him, as it is for many of us, to move from looking outward to turning within.

> *I learned the hard way. There was a long 'wilderness' period in which I sought resources outside myself. I looked for an answer . . . Good years went by. It took a long time for me to discover that the only real answer . . . is to concern myself with the drawing forth of what is uniquely me.*[12]

There is something that is paradoxical in how turning toward our own uniqueness can help us serve others. Great humility is needed in learning what we have to give and learning to use it more fully. Ann often shares about how Robert Greenleaf continually affirmed her uniqueness. The following is a powerful story from Ann that reminds us why it is so important for us as servant-leader coaches to uncover unique genius in ourselves and our coaching Partners.

| Ann McGee-Cooper

## TURNING TO MY OWN INNER GENIUS

In the spring of 1950, I remember seeing my first exhibition of the work of Vincent Van Gogh in a Houston museum. As I walked out into the spring sunshine amid the blossoms of fruit trees, I remember feeling deeply saddened by the realization that during Van Gogh's lifetime only his brother, Theo, recognized the amazing genius of this incredibly gifted artist. Van Gogh struggled to live and died never enjoying the support and recognition of the general public, yet he was totally committed to his art. This awareness struck a chord deep within me. I vowed that I would do my best to recognize genius early and become an appreciative audience who would encourage emerging genius early, during the lifetime of the artist, architect, or in whatever form the genius might be expressed. A personal calling took root in me and began to direct the course of my life.

I married a man whom I saw as an unrecognized genius and devoted the next seven years to supporting and encouraging his talent. I worked to put him through seminary and typed all his papers, helping frequently with his graduate research. I learned a valuable lesson during this time. My support frightened him because he wasn't ready to express his full genius. He would write or paint, then destroy his work. I would take dictation, type, and retype his seminary papers, only to see him destroy them at the eleventh hour. I had to learn that I had the right to choose to grow and express my genius and that I must respect the freedom of others to make their own choices. As he became more and more destructive, I sought counseling to understand my part in this process. I finally was able to leave a physically abusive marriage, recognizing that I couldn't make decisions for anyone other than myself. I had a responsibility to get both my small son and myself out of a dangerous and abusive situation. I learned that I had become co-dependent, enabling the abusive behavior of another through empathy. Yet I was part of the problem because I did not have the skills to hold him accountable for his behavior. Through this, I learned the shadow side of my own genius.

> **I had the right to grow and express my genius and that I must respect the freedom of others to make their own choices."**

During the next several years, I became a teacher with a special interest in youngsters whom others viewed as hopeless. I was fortunate to be mentored by Wade Thompson, a true servant-leader and the principal of Everett Lee DeGolyer Elementary School. Mr. Thompson believed firmly that every child belonged in our school family, no matter how severe his or her disabilities were. "If they are warm and breathing, it's our responsibility to create a healthy, supportive, loving learning environment. And all the children will be better from helping to support and encourage the least among us. Every child has a gift to share. Let's find those gifts and honor the best in each child."

Mr. Thompson taught me so much about starting from strengths and building on the unique gifts in each child. When it came time for him to retire, I remember him calling me in to help me plan for my future. "Ann, it's time for you to go to the university level and help teach others the creative ways you reach into the lives of each child to awaken the special gifts they have been given." And my reply was, "But I have so much more I need to learn. I'm not ready to teach teachers."

"Ann, let me put it another way. I'm planning to retire in May and I don't think I can find another principal who will fully appreciate your creative approach to teaching. I think it best for you to find a university that will welcome the unique ways you reach even those youngsters who others consider unreachable. You have a gift and a responsibility to teach it to others. Go find a way to recruit more people like you into the teaching profession."

With that charge, I spoke with five universities for whom I had supervised student teachers over the past four years. I chose Southern Methodist University (SMU) because it would allow me to establish a lab school as an innovative way to attract, grow, and develop a different kind of person into the teaching profession.

| Ann McGee-Cooper

## THE STRANDS OF UNDERSTANDING AND GROWING GENIUS

Through two failed marriages, I learned painfully that I couldn't live anyone's genius but my own. I learned painfully about the "Jonah Complex"—running away from one's calling. I learned about the fears of owning one's genius, the depression that comes from keeping a lid on one's calling, and the unmatched and abundant joy that accompanies the courage to unleash one's personal gifts.

At SMU, I founded and directed the Experimental Arts Program, which was a research initiative focused on those youngsters others had given up on. One by one, each lived into their giftedness. Recognized internationally as a unique model of educational excellence, we enhanced the philosophy of Montessori with the belief that every child has the innate creative capacity to express personal genius. Leading educators came from around the world to learn from our work, including the minister of education from Brazil and scores of faculty members from Texas Tech University and Teachers College at Columbia University. Over time, we learned that the most important characteristic for a teacher to qualify to teach in the Talented and

Gifted (TAG) programs was for that teacher to have the courage to claim and live his or her own giftedness. Society typically punishes those who march to their own drummer, and having the empathy to understand the journey of gifted children demands the courage to be on that journey personally.

Lives were transformed in astounding ways! One day, Duane Trammell, then a graduate student and exceptional young teacher in Dallas Independent School District's distinguished TAG program, wondered with me what might happen if we took what we had learned about children and teachers and brought it to business leaders. Once again, the work was richly validated; repeatedly, individual lives made remarkable leaps toward personal genius and calling.

We worked with many dedicated executives such as Bob Gary, then executive vice president of generation at TXU Energy, who had a goal to wake up the creative right brains of his engineering managers. We consulted with Jack Lowe, Sr., CEO and founder of TDIndustries, who was dedicated to co-creating an innovative curriculum teaching servant leadership to Employees at every level of the business. Although many were craft workers with only a high school education, some had advanced degrees in business, engineering, and accounting. This servant leadership program has become uniquely recognized worldwide as one of the most effective in its field.

> "Genius is typically not celebrated until it is safely dead for many years."

As I looked at all of these things, I didn't fully realize how these strands had come together so elegantly, each bringing value and new insight to all the others. When I claimed some quiet solitude for several days to reflect on the meaning of the journey into genius and my own personal vision, mission, and calling, synchronicity began to tap on my shoulder and hold up this mirror, helping me to see how everything in my life has contributed to preparing me to do this work. Our strengths come from all directions and flow into elegant patterns, each making the next stronger, like weaving a French braid. For me this is spiritual work. I view the unique gift given to each of us as a divine gift, along with the expectation that we have the courage to embrace our uniqueness and through it give back to the world. This takes extraordinary courage because society will do its darnedest to keep each of us conveniently complying with the status quo and not coloring outside the lines. Genius is typically not celebrated until it is safely dead for many years. My goal is to change this and encourage those around me to dare to live their personal genius and to inspire others to do the same. When we become our best selves, we enjoy extraordinary energy, and often when we least expect it, the world opens up to support us.

| Deborah Welch

## HAVING THE COURAGE TO EMBRACE OUR OWN GENIUS

I am touched by Ann's story every time I read it. She illustrates how reflecting on one's unique gifts over the course of myriad experiences helped her realize how her genius has been working through many different life phases. By reflecting on how these relate to her life purpose, she uncovers a way to claim the use of her genius in bolder ways—ways that are more energizing and lead her to make greater contributions when she serves others. Another message from her story is that servant-leaders sometimes have a tendency to ignore our own gifts. In my desire to serve others, I can easily forget that ignoring my own talents doesn't help others; in fact, I limit my ability to be most helpful to others. After coaching hundreds of people on finding their strengths and genius, I see how this tendency to misperceive, misunderstand, or disown our gifts can happen. We misunderstand true humility and think that it means to keep ourselves small. Actually, humility is more about getting the ego out of the way to let the greatness that we have inside ourselves be unleashed because then we can be of greatest service to others.

As a coach it is vital to develop greater self-awareness and expand confidence in our own core strengths. As we do this for ourselves, we can do it for others when we coach. We learn to pay attention to what lights up Clients or Partners and energizes them and then to help them reflect on how they can best learn and grow. For example, in my interview with Dawna she shared how when she works with a coaching Client who is highly kinesthetic she adjusts the way she coaches so that their work together is maximized.

## COACHING UNIQUE LEARNING STYLES AND TALENTS | Dawna Markova

IN WORKING WITH ONE CEO, we learned from *The Smart Navigator®* assessment that his brain uses auditory information in the left hemisphere, kinesthetic information in both sides, and visual information in the right hemisphere. When we can't be together, if I talk to Peter using Skype he stares at me, his pupils dilate, and the visual information triggers him into this kind of "Duh!" state of "I can't get through." He's there, but he's in a trance. He's right-hemisphere functioning. When he gives a speech, he paces back and forth. The kinesthetic movement energizes his brain, and he uses words that are very precise, powerful, and energized in the way Bill Clinton does. He and I communicate much better when we go for a walk or when he talks with me on the phone with earphones in and he walks. Then he's fully alert. When we stop, his kinesthetic energy calms down and he describes what he's seeing, and we can make a connection.

| Deborah Welch

## LEARNING STYLES AND WHAT LIGHTS US UP

Dawna's use of an assessment and her keen observation to learn how to work with each Partner's gifts and talents illustrates several key principles for servant-leader coaching. First, she is attending to Peter's learning style. She honors how movement activates his kinesthetic intelligence. To understand how our coaching Partners learn may take time, observation, and many good conversations. Additionally, Dawna is recognizing and lifting up greatness. There are many ways we can use assessments and tools to identify talents, but beyond that, there is paying attention to what lights up an individual. When Robert Greenleaf coached, he attended in a deeply respectful way to the intuition and gifts of others. He listened for Ann's gifts when he coached her and noticed what lit her up.

Parker Palmer also writes about this using different words but conveying the same message of encouragement to help those we care about find their special gifts.

## BIRTHRIGHT GIFTS | Parker Palmer

IF YOU DOUBT THAT WE ALL ARRIVE in this world with gifts, pay attention to an infant or a very young child. A few years ago, my daughter and her newborn baby came to live with me for a while. I was able, in my early fifties, to see something that had eluded me as a twenty-something parent: my granddaughter arrived in the world as *this* kind of person rather than that, or that, or that. She did not show up as raw material to be shaped into whatever image the world might want her to take. She arrived with her own gifts. I began observing the inclinations and proclivities that were planted in her at birth. I noticed, and I still notice, what she likes and dislikes, what she is drawn toward and repelled by, how she moves, what she does, what she says.

I am gathering my observations in a letter. When my granddaughter reaches her late teens or early twenties, I will make sure that my letter finds its way to her, with a preface something like this: "Here is a sketch of who you were from your earliest days in this world. It is not a definitive picture—only you can draw that. But it was sketched by a person who loves you very much. Perhaps these notes will help you do sooner something your grandfather did only later: remember who you were when you first arrived and reclaim the gift of true self."

We arrive in this world with birthright gifts. Then, as young people, we are surrounded by expectations that may have little to do with who we really are.[13]

| Deborah Welch

## RECLAIMING OUR SPECIAL GIFTS

Parker Palmer goes on to explain how many of us begin to reclaim our gifts especially in the second half of life. Although there may be a myth that individuals reach adulthood fully mature, many of us grow into our most authentic and best selves in the second half of our lives, far beyond what we might have imagined when we were younger. Robert Greenleaf once said, "Think of yourself as a person with unique potentialities." He emphasized that an important purpose in life is to "bring these into mature bloom." And indeed, much of the work of a servant-leader coach is to do just this.

Great servant-leader coaches believe in those they serve, looking for the gifts in others in the same way Parker Palmer did this for his granddaughter. Sometimes it is important to lift those talents up, and this can take courage on the part of the servant-leader coach.

In our conversation with Matt Kosec, he reflects on honoring the talents of others in this way.

### HAVE YOU HEARD OF VIVIEN THOMAS? | Matt Kosec

FOR WHATEVER REASON, there are times that we suppress our own strengths and genius. The best coaches encourage those to emerge. Sometimes, however, it is external circumstances and situations that prevent our gifts from surfacing.

Consider Vivien Thomas. While there's little doubt he would be Dr. Vivien Thomas in today's age, his medical genius was suppressed by racial segregation in the U.S. in the1940s. Thomas quietly assisted Dr. Alfred Blalock at Vanderbilt University. Blalock, however, eventually disregarded social norms by recognizing Thomas's uncanny medical knowledge. Despite fierce opposition from his peers, Blalock helped Thomas to develop into a medical practitioner who is now celebrated in textbooks as a pioneer of cardiac surgery.

The servant-leader coach encourages and grows the mentee's strengths and genius, regardless of the situation and occasionally at some organizational risk. He or she understands that genius is something worthy to be celebrated.

| Deborah Welch

### BRINGING WHAT ENERGIZES OUR PARTNER INTO AWARENESS

Celebrating the strengths of Partners, noticing what energizes them, and aligning goals and tasks with talents can bring strengths into much greater use in the organization. Here is the way Howard Behar put it in coaching leaders at Starbucks:

*When our passions become clear, our strengths and goals come more sharply into focus. Over a lifetime, we all learn skills, improve, change direction, and work to moderate our flaws. But our natural talents give us the energy we need to persist in achieving the goals and results we seek. If a goal is not working for you, you're not connected to it. Raise it, make it meaningful, make it touch something in you that you want. Or take it off your list.*[14]

When we think about how to align goals and roles with one's talents through coaching, it is also important to consider the starting point. The work of partnering or coaching to uplift strengths can be done with one person in an organization. It can be even more powerful to have a partnership of two within the organization do this work together because it can create an island of support within a culture that is not yet supporting an initiative. Ideally, a whole leadership team could be involved in a coaching initiative that could be tiered out to reach others. This story from Shaunna Black illustrates what happens when a leader brings a coaching initiative to all the Partners on a team. It's a gift that unleashes the talents of each member and enhances the culture and offers business results.

## THE POWER OF SERVANT LEADERSHIP COACHING FOR TEAMS | Shaunna Black

IN 2007, I WAS VICE PRESIDENT of a global division representing 1,500 people in a Fortune 500 technology company. We were responsible for the construction, operation, and maintenance of facilities in twenty-five countries; implementation of environmental, safety, and health programs; the company's sustainability strategy; and corporate real estate. I supported a leadership team of twelve people responsible for the success and welfare of this division. Our team was a high trust, collaborative, global team with a reputation for high performance. However, we worked in a very competitive industry and knew we had to continually grow our capabilities and competencies if we wanted to sustain our top performance. In addition, our company continued to expand our operations globally, so we were constantly integrating new team members worldwide. We valued continuous improvement and had a desire to provide a culture and framework for our organization that would unleash the full potential of our people, strategies, and programs.

Our department managers were selected because they were natural servant-leaders. They were collaborative, inclusive, embracing of differences, and had a service mindset. We had never utilized the formal concept of servant leadership in our organization. It was not a label which was commonly used in the technology industry, and frankly, it made some leaders on our team uncomfortable. However, there came a time when we decided that using the formal framework of servant leadership could be a catalyst for debate and dialogue to develop the kind of culture that we would design together. We wanted to send a clear message that we were committed to grow our culture and to back it up by offering coaching as a gift to everyone on the leadership team. For many of our team members, this was the first formal executive coaching they had ever received, and they valued it as a precious gift from our company. They found coaching to be transforming.

One of the most valuable things I learned about coaching was how to listen deeply with a presence and loving acceptance—how to create a safe environment where others could grow as persons and as leaders. Ann McGee-Cooper, who coached all team members, including myself, exemplified these attributes. She listened with a presence and loving acceptance I had never experienced previously. I learned from her that a great coach listens for the spirit and the heart and the unspoken longings waiting to be voiced rather than just the context or the content. She was a guide and a Partner on my journey. We unwound the mystery of who I am together, which was often accompanied by laughter or tears. Ann enabled me to celebrate the ways I was using my genius but also helped me notice where I wasn't maximizing my gifts. Coaching freed me to explore why I was reluctant to step fully into my genius, what blocked me from being my authentic self, and what I could do to achieve my deeply desired vision of my future. I began to see the beauty in my genius and how to unleash my gifts and talents without being overpowering. A journey into self-knowledge can be very challenging, emotional, and revealing. People open their heart and soul, exposing their innermost secrets. It is an exciting but challenging experience. I learned to suspend my self-judgment and

> **"A great coach listens for the spirit and the heart and the unspoken longings waiting to be voiced."**

become curious, enabling me to truly explore and understand my unique, powerful, authentic self. I began to work in more of a state of flow. My coach was a powerful mirror for me, allowing me to better see my beliefs, my values, my gifts, my talents, and my dreams. She believed that what I bring to the world is unique and truly extraordinary and that I'm capable of greatness in my calling. As a result, I was able to bring these practices into the way I coached my leadership team.

Our leadership team learned to be curious together and explore new ways of thinking and leading, which significantly impacted our performance as a team and as an organization. We operated more collaboratively and synergistically by using the genius of each member.

Collectively, we designed an encouraging, supportive culture beyond our expectations that positively impacts the lives of our global team members. The freedom we all experienced was transforming. We learned to be loving and nonjudgmental; to be curious, looking beyond the obvious; to be aware of unintended consequences; and to increase our ability to quickly change direction to achieve our goals. Together, we learned to use our individual and collective genius more fully to create the path to our shared vision. Along with the development of a servant leadership culture came many business results, such as

- Attained $10 million annualized savings globally

- Achieved the best safety record in the Semiconductor Industry Association (SIA) for five consecutive years and reduced waste to 5 percent of resources purchased

- Led a corporate sustainability strategy, saving $12 million in annualized utility savings and completed $605 million capital projects including a 1.1 million square-foot wafer fabrication facility (Gold Leadership in Energy and Environmental Design certified), the first LEED-certified factory in the U.S., along with the first LEED-certified facility in Asia

| Deborah Welch

## HELPING OTHERS BY EMBRACING OUR OWN GREATNESS

Shaunna had the courage to risk and grow, to take on coaching and infuse it throughout her organization's culture. This is a great example of living up to extraordinary potential. When she says, "*I began to see the beauty in my genius and how to unleash my gifts and talents without being overpowering,*" there is a lot behind what it takes to accomplish this. And although in some organizations coaching is used for remediation to fix people's problems, as Shaunna points out, coaching is better offered as a gift to each team member. Finally, this story illustrates how servant-leaders investing in people results in great financial return. This coaching initiative can be measured in "triple-bottom-line" results—good for people, the planet, and profit. This story explains how all the leaders on the team benefited along with those they served. One example of contributions to the planet that were made through this initiative was having the first factory to be certified by LEED, a certification that ensures standards have been met for reducing the negative environmental impacts of buildings. Strong profits came as a result. There can be a misconception that servant-leaders do not attend to business results, but that is far from the truth. It's just that they know clearly that profits come as a result of a high-performing culture. In his book *Firms of Endearment: How World-Class Companies Profit from Passion and Purpose*, Rajendra Sisodia writes:

> *[Some people believe that] the purpose of business is to make as much money as possible. That's like saying that because we need red blood cells to live, the purpose of life is to make red blood cells. . . . Great business leaders channel their employees' desires to be a part of something bigger than themselves and to be a part of making the world a better place for their children into the overall purpose of their business. Profit is an outcome.*[15]

> **❝There can be a misconception that servant-leaders do not attend to business results, but that is far from the truth.❞**

## REFLECTIONS

At the end of each chapter, there are questions for reflection that we have found to be helpful for servant leadership coaching. There is also a chart in appendix A called "Coaching with a Servant's Heart." You will find ideas from this chapter summarized in the chart. To apply the ideas, you may use the chart or consider one of these questions to explore how to take your own coaching work further:

**1** *Knowing my own strengths stories can be helpful in coaching others. Do I have a story of a strength that I once disowned? What have I learned since then? How do I make time to identify and grow my own gifts, strengths, or genius? What story might I share with someone I am coaching?*

**2** *In what ways can I, as a servant-leader coach, continue to grow in understanding what lights me up?*

**3** *As a servant-leader coach, how do I find ways to identify and lift up what lights up those I serve?*

*Note:* As you read these questions and throughout this book, you can use the word *gift* or *strength* or *genius*—whichever word fits best for you. We use all three words to represent the unique potentials of each individual.

# 2

# COACHING THROUGH STORIES: SERVANT LEADERSHIP COACHING AS MUTUAL DISCOVERY

MUCH OF THE WORK OF servant leadership coaching is about growing as a person. To grow as a person requires something very different than advice giving. It requires self-awareness and reflection. As we look at the process of growing our unique gifts and strengths, sharing stories can be a powerful tool for coaches. We want to approach a coaching time with a spirit of reflection and a focus for learning, and that often means breaking out of the overly busy, 500-tasks-in-front-of-me, linear-thinking mentality. Other times, it may be letting go of something that made it hard to sleep the night before. Stories create a change in our perspective and in the way we think.

A good story paints a picture that can pivot our thinking toward knowing ourselves better and toward discovering new possibilities. There are many kinds of stories that are useful in coaching. Some are parables that have been passed down through the years. Some are from wisdom figures in our lives. A movie we have seen may have a message which deepens our ideas about servant leadership and our awareness of how to grow as a servant-leader. Oftentimes it is sharing a story from our own experience that is the most helpful to those we are serving.

***In this chapter, we will explore***

1. *How coaches can use stories to express empathy, relating with people by sharing difficult experiences*

2. *How coaches can use stories to share lessons learned from mistakes*

3. *How coaches can help Partners "rewrite" their stories when the stories aren't serving them well*

4. *How coaches can use their own personal stories to forge deep collective connections*

5. *How coaches can be sensitive to "the other story" when hero stories are told in organizations*

| Ann McGee-Cooper

## STORIES CAN TAKE US INTO A DIFFERENT WAY OF THINKING

Robert Greenleaf had the gift of telling stories. He would listen to me but then tell a story, and sometimes I'd think he hadn't heard me and was going off in a different direction. Years later, I realized he was helping me think in a different way through stories. It was his way of helping me *slow down* to see what I hadn't seen. It would take me into my own life journey.

Cynthia Watson relates a story she used in the workplace about how she got through a difficult time on her servant leadership journey.

## USING STORIES IN THE WORKPLACE | Cynthia Watson

AS A MANAGER, I HAVE OFTEN had the opportunity to tell my story. Just recently, I was conducting interviews for a first-line manager position in our organization. The group of applicants was young and enthusiastic. At the conclusion of one of the interviews, one candidate asked me why I went into management. I shared with him that I worked full time as a single parent with two children while getting my undergraduate degree. I started college with the idea that I would go into teaching and worked toward this goal. During the semester that I was student teaching, life intervened; both of my children caught chicken pox, and I became very ill with bronchial pneumonia. I was forced to withdraw from school. Because I could not work and also student teach, I did not have the financial resources to repeat my student teaching the next semester. If that was not bad enough, the relationship that I was in also ended about the same time. It was a real low point in my life. So, I found another job as a clerk-typist with the power company. I was grateful to have a job with health insurance benefits and relatively decent pay for that line of work. Fortunately for me, the manager I went to work for was a wonderful human being. He encouraged me to go back and complete my college education. He allowed me the opportunity to study at work if there was a lull or when I was caught up with my duties, and he allowed me to use my vacation hours on an intermittent basis to attend two classes that were not offered at night. Without his support and his bending the rules a bit, it is likely that I would not have been able to complete my degree.

Once I graduated, I began the career path that led to my current position. After my former manager retired, I lost track of him. For several years I searched for him on the Internet because I wanted to call him and tell him "the rest of the story" and thank him for his confidence and generosity in supporting me. Just this past year, I finally located him and was able to call him. It meant so much to me to be able to share with him how his actions had affected my life and to give him my gratitude. And that is what inspired me to go into management—because I know first-hand the positive influence that managers can have when they use their power wisely.

After I finished telling this story to the applicant and the other two people in the room, there was complete silence. It was one of those rare moments when you could literally feel the connection, and you knew that something powerful was happening. Finally, one of the other managers in the room said, "You know, you should really tell these types of stories more often so people can see that there is another side to you. They see you as you are now, not when you were going through the early struggles of the journey." Maybe that is part of the value of stories from leaders in organizations—to help others see that we have faced challenges too.

> **One of the most reliable indicators of leadership is the ability to find meaning in negative events."**

| Deborah Welch

## STORIES HELP US KNOW OURSELVES BETTER

One of the things Cynthia did when she told her story to the group that day was to recall a defining moment in her own learning and the values she wanted to pass on in her own leadership role. She had felt challenged to her core, and this mentor who invested in her helped her get through it. Warren Bennis would call this a "leadership crucible" story, a common story that research shows is often told by extraordinary leaders. He says, "Everyone is tested by life, but only a few extract strength and wisdom from the most trying experiences. ...One of the most reliable indicators of true leadership is an individual's ability to find meaning in negative events and to learn from even the most trying circumstances."[16] So, in the midst of challenge there may be a defining moment, a *crucible* moment when we put our ego aside, find our way through adversity, and invest ourselves in what matters most.

I often think of the story Steve Jobs told to a Stanford University graduating class about the time that he was fired from his own organization. He said,

> *I was a very public failure, and I even thought about running away from the Valley. But something slowly began to dawn on me—I still loved what I did. The turn of events at Apple had not changed that one bit. I had been rejected, but I was still in love. And so I decided to start over. ... I didn't see it then, but it turned out that getting fired from Apple was the best thing that could have ever happened to me. The heaviness of being successful was replaced by the lightness of being a beginner again, less sure about everything. It freed me to enter one of the most creative periods of my life.*[17]

The Steve Jobs story reminds me to follow the work I love and the possibility of working with lightness, even when conditions might feel humiliating. Cynthia's story helps me remember the times in my life when an extraordinary mentor helped me at a pivotal moment in time. In both cases, I feel less alone knowing of the humanness of others on a leadership journey. Another thing that happens in Cynthia's story is that she is surprised to learn how much her listeners appreciate seeing her humanness. This touched on a depth of empathy that happens through sharing stories as a servant-leader coach. Consider one more story that illustrates this from Rebecca Braden.

## OUR OWN STORIES OF MISTAKES CAN BE "PREAMBLES" FOR DIFFICULT CONVERSATIONS | Rebecca Braden

ONE OF THE "GIFTS" OF HAVING twenty-five years of experience working with leaders and aspiring leaders (primarily in the technology sector) is that I have catalogued countless mistakes! I often share with groups I work with that I have unintentionally offended people on every continent except Antarctica (which is true!). This actually comes in handy when I am coaching aspiring servant-leaders. I find that when I am in a position of providing feedback that may be difficult or embarrassing for my coachee to hear, if I can reach into my repertoire of stories about parallel experiences I have had, it makes it easier for him/her to hear the feedback. Then I can support my coachee in determining what action might need to be taken.

Not long ago, when I was working with the IT group in a Fortune 500 company, a young director who had been with the company for a little over a year did not attend the funeral of a woman in his part of the organization who had been with the company for over twenty years. Several people had sought me out as a "neutral listener" to talk about how deeply it had hurt those closest to her when their leader did not show up at the service. They felt like he had ignored the grief so many were feeling. He was "silent" and "not visible" for about a week after the funeral and then began to redistribute the work that needed to be covered to the rest of the team. Of course, this all felt very cold and uncaring to the people on the team.

When all of this was described to me, I was really surprised. I knew this young man to be very committed to his journey as a servant-leader, and I knew he genuinely cared for his people. This behavior seemed very uncharacteristic of the person I knew him to be. I was certain that this was just a horrible oversight on his part. The senior manager who worked most directly with the team would have been the "right" person to provide this feedback to him, but she was feeling emotionally shattered and very angry by his behavior. I knew he needed to hear how people were feeling. So I arranged a meeting with him, but I really agonized about how to tee up this feedback. In the wee hours of a pretty sleepless night before our meeting, it dawned on me how I could preamble what I would share with him.

> 66 **Parallel experiences make it easier to hear feedback."**

I told this director a story about a time when I was doing a workshop in Kuala Lumpur and one of the graphics on a PowerPoint slide in my presentation was a pig. Malaysia is a Muslim nation. I knew that Muslims didn't eat pork, but I had *no idea* that even a picture of a pig was very offensive to them. There were about a half-dozen Muslims in my class, and none of them said anything about the slide. After the class, a Chinese manager approached me graciously and politely said that he had really enjoyed the workshop and learned a lot. Then he asked if it would be okay if he gave me some constructive feedback. Of course, I invited him to please share his observations. When he explained the situation, I was horrified, but because he had had the courage to let me know about my mistake, I was able to contact each of the Muslim participants and apologize for my ignorance. Every single person was very gracious and accepted my apology. I told the young director that I was sharing this story with him because he had committed a similar faux pas, and I wanted to let him know so he could decide how to address the situation.

As it turned out, this director had a family emergency to deal with at the same time his employee passed away. He naively assumed that the senior manager of the team, who was much closer than he was both to the deceased and to those who experienced the loss most deeply, would shepherd these employees through this loss. Unfortunately, he had not understood the importance of his own presence or his expression of sympathy, and he was completely oblivious to the impact of all of this on his people.

As I had known he would be, he felt embarrassed and terrible about his oversight, but he was grateful that I had let him know. He thanked me for sharing my experience—how that had made him realize what a gift it was to know what he had done (or not done) so he could try to make it right.

Sharing my own embarrassing stories as a preamble in situations like this one often opens the door for coachees to be vulnerable and work through their emotions without shame or defensiveness.

| Deborah Welch

## STORIES CAN EXTEND EMPATHY

Rebecca's story reminds me that we are all human and imperfect, and we all undergo big and little humiliations and missteps. Even so, there are ways to recover when a mistake is made. Trust is not always destroyed. The empathy conveyed through a story can go deeper than any idea or tool we might have available as coaches.

An additional point is that not all stories are helpful in servant leadership coaching. There are victim stories and other misguided stories that we tell ourselves. Some of the work of sharing our stories is to work with them in a way that enables us to know our best selves and our strengths better. As David Drake puts it, "Over time some stories are no longer salient or defining, and others take on a more defining nature as we come to know ourselves better."[18] When coaching, we aim for ways to help our Partners shift toward stories that better represent who they are at their best, for a storytelling voice that comes from deeper wisdom in understanding who they are and how they want to react in any given situation. The quality of a story matters. An awareness of the tone of the story makes it more meaningful to the one listening.

> **66**
> **..the stories we tell ourselves and others influence the future to a high degree."**

In a workshop by Peter Senge and Betty Sue Flowers called "New Stories to Shape the Future," they pointed out that the stories we tell ourselves and others influence the future to a high degree. Then they asked all the participants to tell their life story as a victim story, a hero story, or a learning story. To tell the story differently, certain facts are selected and built on toward a particular conclusion.[19] When we get stuck in a victim story, we may stay stuck until we examine the story, discern fact from fiction, or go down the *Ladder of Inference*. (For more on the Ladder of Inference tool, see chapter 5.) When we begin to free ourselves from an old story that may not be true or serving us well, we can see new possibilities.

| Ann McGee-Cooper

## MUTUAL LEARNING AND REWRITING OUR STORIES

Listening to how I tell myself what is happening around me is a key to self-actualization. In my stories, am I a victim with no power to make things happen? Am I at the mercy of traffic, the weather, my upbringing, or of those around me? Or do I see life as a gift and discover that I create the quality of my life? Viktor Frankl awakened me to the power of my choices in his riveting book *Man's Search for Meaning*.[20] He told about what he learned during his more than four years in German concentration camps during World War II. What kept people alive was not what he first thought, optimum health and physical strength. Instead, it was hope and a compelling purpose for life beyond the present. Even in the most difficult circumstances, we can choose to find hope and purpose. And this becomes transforming.

In servant leadership coaching, it is important to be in the conversation in a deeply respectful way. The theologian Martin Buber first introduced me to reflecting on how I related to others, learning to respect the sacredness of each person, not as an *it* (an object to be used) or even a *you* (a person separate from me) but rather as a *thou* (a sacred other) with whom we can discover more of the sacred mystery of life and our personal and collective calling. Dialogue is a way of being in conversation in order to discover meaning and to become curious about what is not readily seen or understood. In dialogue, we learn to replace opinion with questions and to use silence to invite new discoveries and fresh awareness. We expect to see life from a new perspective and therefore to make wonderful creative breakthroughs. Two key questions that form a foundation for servant leadership coaching dialogue are

1.   How can problems become transformational opportunities?

2.   What am I doing or not doing to feed the problem I don't want?

In the spirit of dialogue, I often share my own early victim stories and how I learned to reframe my challenges within a much larger scope of opportunities. I often talk about fears that I confront, ways I have tried in the past to cover my stumbling, and times that I labeled and blamed others and learned to change.

Having the courage to reveal my shadow, learning how to avoid letting my strengths overplay into dysfunction, and sharing my flawed journey is something Clients consistently tell me is very helpful to them. And telling these stories seems to create the safety for a much deeper I/Thou dialogue.

Here is one example of how a Client grew to discover more of her strengths through story sharing and dialogue. I asked her to write the story of her experience, but first let me tell you that this professional woman was the youngest member of her firm of, at that time, thirty Partners. I realized three years ago that she was caught in victim stories along with three of her colleagues and sensed that she would be open to learning if approached respectfully. And she was. With each conversation she took courageous action and appreciated my honesty, which was not always comfortable for her to hear. For example, early on she would get very worked up about certain situations, so much so that the negative stories she was telling herself caused her to suffer physically, limiting her life and performance. I suggested that she was telling herself stories which fueled her getting worked up and gave her examples of how she could choose to tell herself different, positive, optimistic, and hopeful stories. She immediately began to practice this different way of thinking. She discovered that by rewriting her story and changing her related self-talk, she no longer needed to use pharmaceuticals to treat physical symptoms. She was delighted. She grew in self-awareness and optimism in writing her own story, in spite of a serious accident and extended hospitalization. She continues to practice her skills and grow. Just recently she took a significant role professionally, taking the lead in writing a very important piece of Customer communication that received high praise from the chairman and chief editor. As a result, she is being mentored by the chairman and given significant new responsibilities that will stretch her professional competencies and open many new career opportunities. She is thankful for consistently positive time with family members and is enjoying her personal life at a new level of confidence and freedom.

I asked her if she would share about our coaching relationship and what has helped her change her story. She offered this reflection:

> *Ann, when we first met, I remember being struck by your ease and curiosity. You just let me talk. You'd only interject to ask clarifying questions and repeat back what I said to make sure you captured everything. You were so thorough, intent, and focused on me. You helped me have the courage to explore different ideas and challenge assumptions. When I nervously expressed interest in exploring a topic, you didn't say, "Wonderful, here are six books I want you to read, do these exercises, and let me know how it goes. Good luck!" You wanted to learn with me and go through this journey together. You continued to ask questions instead of giving me answers or telling me I needed to change or that I needed to suck it up and get over myself. You made me feel safe to slowly start letting my guard down, knowing that I wasn't going to be forced to do anything I wasn't ready to do. And you didn't seem to pass*

*any judgment. You were gentle yet persistent, respectful of my aversion to change. You didn't make me feel slow or stupid for not moving forward at your pace. There was unusual reciprocity in our coaching relationship. You shared and made yourself vulnerable to me. The outcome was twofold: it invited me to do the same, and it helped me form a connection with you.*

*When my grandfather died you showed me how I could use that time to support my dad and work on my relationship with him. Or after I was hospitalized myself, you helped me not fall into victim mode. Instead, you showed me how to stay positive and look for opportunities to learn and grow. Also, you've never pretended like you have all the answers—that you have everything figured out. It's intimidating and a bit condescending when people do that. It makes me feel like something's wrong with me, especially when I'm admitting that I'm struggling and need help. You made yourself vulnerable and shared what was on your heart. Most of our moments together were not glamorous moments—they were vulnerable,*

> **"You planted a seed that made me want to figure out what my gifts were."**

*raw, pure, authentic moments that spoke beyond words. You helped give me the courage to explore the scary shadow parts of my life, and you created a safe place for me to journal through our email exchanges and conversations.*

*It took a lot of unlearning and letting go of numerous worn out mental models and old stories for me to transition out of a victim mentality. It wasn't easy, but you graciously listened as I discovered how deep a hole I had dug myself into. I have realized that most of what I believed and most of my identity was associated with what I've been told instead of what I discovered on my own.*

*It took a while to accept how much time and energy you were devoting to me and to believe that I might have something to offer. As I began to let go of my negative story and the mental models and beliefs underneath it, you helped open my eyes to see that I wasn't living up to my potential. You planted a seed and instilled a curiosity in me that made me want to figure out what my gifts were.*

| Deborah Welch

## EVOLVING OUR STORIES

The story we just shared with you illustrates how Ann demonstrated unconditional acceptance and belief in her Client/Partner in a way that was highly mutual and that led her to drop the old stories and embrace her strengths. She slowly found her way to a truer story, one that highlights her greatest strengths and gifts. We can rewrite the stories we tell ourselves at any time, but the process does not happen overnight. It can take us up, down, backward, and sideways. And sometimes we have to stay with a story because understanding the meaning of difficult events doesn't always happen until time passes. As Orson Welles says, "If you want a happy ending, that depends, of course, on where you stop your story."

One final point about the power of stories in servant leadership is that our stories help us know each other. Stories can build bonds, develop trust, and lead us to the greatest meaning in our lives and our work. When I asked Dawna Markova for an illustration of her work partnering with Clients as she coaches, the first thing she did was tell me a powerful story.

## CONNECTION, THE HUMAN SPIRIT,
## AND COLLABORATIVE INTELLIGENCE | Dawna Markova

I WORKED FOR SEVERAL YEARS with a CEO we'll call Peter, who led a company of 200,000 people. We met at a conference in Costa Rica, where I gave a keynote speech that began with this story:

> When I was younger, I read to my father. I read *The Wall Street Journal* as well as all of his correspondence. . . . After I read the papers on his desk I would put my hand under his big old ink blotter. We don't have those things anymore, but he used to have one on his desk. I'd put my hand under the ink blotter, and there would be a quarter. The quarter was for me to get a hot fudge sundae.
>
> My father and I had this very mixed relationship: I was very close to him, but he also had an immense temper. That's what we called it back then. Let's just say he had some issues controlling his rage. When he arrived home each night, my mother had a list

of all the things I had done wrong during the day. My father then spanked me furiously. When that was over, he'd put his hand in his pocket, take out a quarter, and put it in my hand. And I'd say, "Daddy, do you love me? Do you love me?" and he'd say, "Here's a quarter. Don't tell your mother." Whenever I asked my father, "Do you love me?" he would do the same thing. As I grew older, it was a dollar. Still, I'd ask the same question, "Daddy, do you love me?" He'd put a dollar in my hand, pat my hand, and say, "Here's a dollar. Don't tell your mother." I was very persistent. I wanted to hear him say he loved me, but he never would. Always, he'd give the same response, placing a dollar in my hand, and saying "Here's a dollar. Don't tell your mother."

So when I went to college, I stopped asking because, you know, I am persistent but not stupid. Decades later, when he was in his sixties, he had Alzheimer's and was dying. He was locked behind invisible walls that nobody could climb, and there was no way to connect with him. I went to Florida when the doctor told me to come and say my last goodbye. My father was sitting in a room. He used to have these fiery blue eyes, but when I saw him this time, his eyes were very watery and empty. There was no way to connect. What I wanted then, more than anything, was for him to know that I loved him. So I took his face in my hands, and I said, "Daddy, Daddy, I love you." Nothing. Giving up, I put my purse on my shoulder and got ready to leave. As I stood up, an idea popped in my mind. I opened my purse and took out a $5 bill. I opened his hand, closed his palm on the $5 bill, and I said, "Here's $5. Don't tell Mommy." He blinked, then looked directly at me and said, "I love you too, sweetheart." That's the last thing he ever said to me. Since he hadn't said a word to anyone in months that seemed impossible. And yet, sometimes I think our soul stretches beyond the impossible.

I don't tell that story very often, but something moved me to tell it at this Costa Rican conference. When I finished, it was totally silent in the ballroom. People just didn't know what to say. As I was going out the back door, this very tall man with straight hair, cut like a brush on top, approached me. He had tears running down his face as he asked,

"Can I talk to you?" We sat knee-to-knee on a couch in the lobby. He was wearing one of those shirts with a little tennis racket over his heart. As he leaned toward me, he said, "I'm the CEO of Frito-Lay. I need you to help me with my daughter, but also I'd like you to help me with my leadership team."

Our thinking partnership began in that moment. The first thing that I had to help him do was recognize that although his daughter was very much like him, in certain ways she was also very different. He needed to understand how her mind worked and what her gifts and talents were. He described himself as growing up on the streets of the Bronx. Like my father, he was a brilliant salesman who could inspire thousands of people. I said, "If you're willing to learn about how your own mind works and what your particular thinking talents are, then I'll help you learn how you could connect with your daughter as well as your leadership team."

## THINKING TALENTS ARE INDIVIDUALIZED | Dawna Markova

MY COLLEAGUES AND I WORK with executives and their leadership teams. Sometimes we will even work with their family members. Once you begin to understand how each human being thinks in a unique and unpredictable way, you have to give up searching for set formulas. I've been studying the mystery I call *Intellectual Diversity* for fifty years, and I'm still in awe of it, still fascinated by it. A lot of the problems ascribed to many other things—personality conflict, for instance, or low performance—really are a matter of miscommunications caused by those differences. In addition, we don't know how to identify our individual thinking talents, align them with the tasks that we're performing, and collaborate with others who think differently. What I did with Peter was to help him recognize his own thinking talents and how to align them with the ways he was fathering and leading his company.

> 66 ...problems ascribed to many other things are a matter of miscommunications caused by differences."

| Deborah Welch

## STORIES THAT FOSTER TRUST: REMEMBERING THE BIGGER PICTURE

This powerful story speaks in meaningful ways on many different levels. It is worth taking time to pause and reflect. What stirred you as you read Dawna's story? Reflecting on her experience with her father inspires me to consider how I connect with others in ways that matter most. When we want to be truly helpful as servant leadership coaches there are elements of grace and mystery at work in our lives. In Dawna's story there is this synchronous moment with her father when he does something that should have been medically impossible. And after telling this vulnerable story of her own personal struggle, a door opens: an invitation for Peter to awaken something he cares about deeply. Dawna explains this force or connection of the heart that draws a person to this work together with her. She calls it collaborative intelligence—and that is one of the outcomes of a dialogic experience where high trust bonds form and we discover deeper truths together by sharing our stories. The ability to express empathy as a coach can open hearts powerfully through sharing a story that reveals our humanness and enables us to see events with a new perspective.

In a dialogue on using stories in servant leadership, Cynthia Watson added further insights about how stories operate in an organization.

## REWRITING OUR ORGANIZATIONAL STORIES | Cynthia Watson

SOME OF THE LESSONS that I've learned about stories are that they come in many shapes and sizes. In our organization, it is common for managers to share war stories from the time in their career when they were investigators. Often this is the "hero's journey" type of story in which the investigator went into a business and met with a very resistant employer. Ultimately, the investigator resolves the issues and recovers back pay for workers in the business. Since the story is told from the perspective of the investigator, he or she becomes the hero in the story. I have often wondered what the corresponding story would be told from the employer's perspective. I think once we realize that we can rewrite our stories, we are moving to a higher level. This is true for organizations as well as for individuals. In every organization there are numerous stories that circulate about the culture, who we are, and what we do. As leaders who want to move organizations forward, we often have to rewrite the story to capture what we are trying to do. In other words, it is the difference between the worker who tells himself that he is just laying bricks and the worker who tells himself that he is building a great cathedral. It is a method of creating vision and building corporate culture within an organization. The corporate culture is directly tied to the stories (official and unofficial versions) in an organization.

| Deborah Welch

## STORIES THAT SERVE A PURPOSE

We can rewrite the collective story in our organizations. And, we can rewrite our personal stories. Sharing our leadership crucible stories is a beginning step. However, here are some caveats and side roads with story sharing. It is important to keep in mind your purpose: to first serve the other person and to share from the right state of heart.

### CAVEATS FOR STORY SHARING | Cynthia Watson

IN A COACHING SITUATION, I think there has to be a real awareness of the difference between listening to the person who is working through a personal situation as opposed to telling your own story. I have become very conscious of not wanting to shift the focus to me. I have learned that there is real value in just listening and using questions rather than interjecting my story at some junctures. I have to be very careful that I don't take the role of "fixer." I have learned that depriving people of struggling with their situations is not always a gift because it can deprive them of the very lessons they are trying to learn. There is value in the struggle, and I can say from personal experience that sometimes I have to come to the end of myself before I am willing to open up and consider other options when I am struggling. There is a lot to be learned about mutual learning in the coaching relationship.

| Deborah Welch

## SHOWING FAITH IN A PARTNER'S LEARNING PROCESS

There are many insights for servant leadership coaching that we can gain from Cynthia's story. One is that we often grow through struggle, and great servant leadership coaching is not about fixing another person but rather recognizing the dignity and spirit of one's coaching Partner and providing mirroring to help the Partner see and choose.

**"It is the difference between the worker who tells himself that he is just laying bricks and the worker who tells himself that he is building a great cathedral."**

## REFLECTIONS

The "Coaching with a Servant's Heart" chart in appendix A provides items that may be used to apply principles from this chapter. To apply guiding ideas from this chapter, consider the following questions:

**1** *Was there a story here that was meaningful for you? Did it remind you of one of your own learning experiences?*

**2** *Has someone shared a learning story with you that impacted you in a way that helped you grow? What did it mean to you?*

**3** *How well do you know your own leadership crucible stories? Is there one you might share?*

**4** *As a coach, how can you use a story to help someone open up to new ways of thinking or to consider how to apply principles to a difficult situation?*

**5** *Can you think of a personal story where you started by telling yourself a victim story and then discovered opportunities to take ownership and turn the problem into an opportunity for personal growth?*

CHAPTER

# GROWING STRONG BONDS IN RELATIONSHIPS

WE LEARN A GREAT DEAL through telling stories that help us discover and use our gifts and strengths. Strength assessments such as the *Herrmann Brain Dominance Instrument*® or *Strengthsfinder*® are a great place to launch into identification of strengths. But this is only a beginning. Strengths development can easily be short-lived if we don't also learn to use our gifts in harmonious ways in relationships. We don't develop our capacities in isolation. The importance of partnering with others who help us see our strengths and possibilities can't be underestimated.

This chapter includes stories that are helpful to someone we are coaching, or to ourselves, to help us grow strong relational bonds. Consider what you already know about what it takes to build powerful relationships—the kind that do not break down but provide support during challenging times. In this chapter, we explore how coaches can grow these kinds of high quality relationships. We talk about a commitment to grow relationships that are centered in dignity and where differences between individuals serve to strengthen our partnerships.

*In this chapter, we will explore four key points concerning how to coach using a Partner's strengths to develop stronger relationships.*

1. *Coaches can align talents and tasks to enhance team capacity.*

2. *Coaches can help Partners use differences to strengthen relationships and results.*

3. *When challenged, coaches can ask, "How can the problem be transformed into an opportunity for greatness?"*

4. *Coaches can model that the relationship with one's "self" is the bedrock of all our relationships.*

**The importance of partnering with others who help us see our strengths and possibilities can't be underestimated."**

The following stories from our various contributors demonstrate how, through coaching, we can find ways to support the best that is possible between people. First, Dawna tells us more of her story coaching the CEO, Peter. In the previous chapter, we were introduced to the story of how Dawna met Peter and how he began to identify his talents and gifts. Now Dawna shares about what happened as Peter and other CEOs used *The Smart Navigator*® assessment to work with their strengths across the leadership team.

## ALIGNING TASKS WITH TALENTS: AN INTERVIEW | Dawna Markova

**Dawna:** When we work with a team, we map the intellectual capacity of the entire team. We can look up their preferred modes of thinking and ascertain who needs analytic input and who needs to see the data first, then teach them cost effective ways of communicating information among themselves—in this case, charts of their numbers before discussions. If you went to a foreign country, you'd learn to translate essential phrases into their language, read important road signs, etc. Every human being is a foreign country! *The Smart Navigator*® helps in this translation process, whether it's between individuals, teams, or whole organizations. Most of my work, at least in the last thirty years, has been with senior leadership teams and CEOs. They're not really interested in concepts. They have to know, "Do I have the right person in the right job?" And if I have this guy who's the head of sales, how do I make sure he knows how to communicate in the mind pattern of the customer? Can he tell stories? Who does he need on this leadership team? What if he has no procedural capacity? Who can he lean on that does so we don't mess up?

**Deborah:** *And so what would we see if we were looking in and were able to see how this all starts to work for the CEO—looking in and now you're using your assessment tool? You're working with him on his relationship with his talents, and it's starting to happen in the organization. Is there anything you could describe about what starts to happen?*

**Dawna:** Well, very often the first thing a CEO recognizes is that he or she has hired people who think just like they do. They've unconsciously created an entire orchestra of violins, even if the company is supposed to function like a marching band. Fifty violins marching up and down a football field doesn't work. Another leader might recognize that she has no relational thinking whatsoever. She doesn't "get" people and is much more talented in the rational than the relational. She might then realize that the most difficult people on her team are, in fact, those who are most concerned with the "who" and least with the "why." Theoretically those leaders might be a perfect complement, but if she doesn't understand intellectual diversity, they will annoy her and seem to always be off topic. We often hear people talk about needing respect. What they don't realize is that for one person, respect may mean sharing information, while for another, it is asking questions.

Much of my work focuses on helping the CEOs and senior leaders understand how to create a very diverse leadership team where they all recognize their own mind patterns and thinking as well as their colleagues' and employees'. Recognizing this helps them achieve a very high-capacity resonance that only diversity can produce. When we grow the conditions where each individual understands what he or she contributes to the whole, when we recognize exactly how we need each other to think the team forward, we function like the unique fingers of a hand. Each has its own unique mark and all are connected to a center that makes a collaborative reach possible.

Peter was a remarkable CEO because he was not only interested in the bottom line but also in developing the talent in each person. This fosters the life force in the organization as a whole. He grows people and they will grow the numbers.

**Deborah:** *This is a level of respecting diversity and a level of collaboration that is—those words are limited compared to what I'm really hearing you say—unstoppable. I'm hearing something beyond synergy. Is it like thriving?*

**Dawna:** It is. It's the way a plant turns towards the light. For example, Deborah, you have this amazing capacity to listen deeply and actively. Some people listen passively. Your listening is very alive. It's like yeast in bread. In our culture, because so many of us have been trained to talk assertively in order to succeed, there is a tremendous connective need for others who can listen generatively.

When we began this phone call, I was tired, burned out. I even wondered why I was taking a call at the end of my day from someone I didn't even know. Once we began and you listened to me in that rich, green way you have, I began telling you stories, which is one of my thinking talents. I woke up. That is not due to me. That is due to the effect you had on me—this yeasting effect that created a collaborative field between us.

When we align with what we are here to do, with that which is a talent that energizes us so effortlessly, we know that we belong, that we matter, that we make a difference. I call that "risking your significance." You are supporting the life force and carried by it in the same way that a small jellyfish is carried by the might of the entire ocean.

| Deborah Welch

## THE CAPACITY FOR HIGH-QUALITY CONNECTIONS

It is powerful to consider how daring we can become when a coach helps us assess strengths, aligns strengths with tasks at hand, creates an environment to support those strengths, and helps Partners find a way to connect to a sense of purpose and what we are truly here for. Duane pinpointed this as "assess, align, support, and dare." This takes great commitment at all levels to reach this potential. However, finding even one coaching Partner and tapping into a deeper knowledge of gifts and strengths and connection to one's purpose is a tremendous step. As Dawna says, there is a great daring that develops, courage that comes from taking time to focus on that which we are really here to do.

> ❝...suddenly there is a rising up of remarkable energy when we combine our strengths and begin to thrive in a relationship."

Reflecting on Dawna's metaphor of yeast in bread, there is synergy from combining two very different elements or two diverse talents when trust is present. This can be a subtle interaction in the beginning, yet suddenly there is a rising up of remarkable energy when we combine our strengths and begin to thrive in a relationship. In my interview with Dawna, I received an exquisite gift in that one hour. As she used her talent for sharing stories, she gave generously, well beyond what I would have imagined. This expanded my listening presence. I don't know if I would have realized how our gifts connected until she pointed it out. Sometimes we don't stop to think about great moments when we uplift each other's talent and the exceptional synergy that results. There are many famous examples throughout history of individuals partnering this way. And when you think of a moment in time of great partnering that you have experienced in your life, you may be able to identify how another person's gifts and talents met your own with great synergy. When this synergy develops over time, remarkable growth and accomplishment happens.

Great coaching is all about fostering this kind of synergy. A synchronized way of working together is sometimes called "collective thriving." Researchers are studying these "high quality relational connections" that are a source of strength for leaders.[21] Great servant leadership coaching involves intentionally seeking out these kinds of partnerships, whether it is inside one's organization, with a friend or a family member, or a coach working with another coach. This is, of course, in contrast to what happens too often in organizations. Relationships can easily be neglected in our 24/7 fast-paced work world.

In the process of learning to uplift each other's gifts, we may encounter many kinds of challenges. Chapter 4 addresses this interference and explores the conflicts and difficulties that can arise because relationships don't develop in a straight line. Often it seems like everything would be great if it weren't for one particular team member. We will examine how we, as coaches, can work with these dynamics. One of the keys we will explore is the way that great coaches listen with an open mind and heart in order to uplift another person's gifts and strengths. Ann calls it strength through difference.

Following are several stories on discovering strength through difference. The first one is told by Duane in his coaching relationship with Nathan Sowell, illustrating the way coaching can be powerful across generational differences.

Duane Trammell

## COACHING ACROSS GENERATIONS

I met Nathan Sowell through his mother, a friend and business colleague. He was twenty-five at the time. In the first five minutes of our meeting, something clicked between us. We saw something that each had to offer the other.

Nathan shared some of his writings with me, which touched a place deep inside me. At first, I thought we would use some of his essays on a business blog. But as he continued to send me material, I believed he needed his own space to publish what he had written. The more he wrote, the more it became clear to me that these essays were telling a story of the inner reflections of a twenty-five-year-old young man.

Nathan's degree and professional training is in finance and accounting, and he works for one of the big financial firms. His daily job as a financial consultant in mergers and acquisitions is an opposite world from the narrative writing he does. Very apparent to me, but not as apparent to him, was that he had a special gift for writing.

> "As coaches, we may doubt ourselves and need a second opinion to confirm the reality of what we are seeing in another's abilities."

Over the past three years, I have helped Nathan recognize his genius (he calls me his muse), and he has helped me understand a new generation of thinkers. As we explored in chapter 1 on "Lifting Up Greatness," there are times we doubt our strengths and gifts. In a recent exchange, Nathan commented on my encouragement of his genius. He said, "You do this with me very well. *So well that I think some of your enthusiasm is contrived.* I try not to consider this possibility. However, you're critical with me often enough to keep this concern at bay." What struck me about this is that often Nathan's first response is to discount positive feedback, and he sometimes feels that I am effusive with flattery about his writing, his ideas, his mind, and his unusual brilliance. I had to ask myself this question: "Am I going overboard in pointing out genius?" I sent a few things that Nathan had written to Don Frick, a good friend who is a published and acclaimed writer. Don immediately wrote back saying,

"Wow, this kid has got it." I respect Don as one of the best writers I know, and he validated what I saw in Nathan. As mentors and coaches, sometimes we may doubt ourselves for a minute and need a second opinion to confirm the reality of what we are sensing, feeling, and seeing in another's abilities.

Our mutual coaching journey has followed the path outlined in "Coaching with a Servant's Heart" (see appendix A). Nathan and I coach each other; it is very non-hierarchical. We recognize and lift up greatness in each other. We pay attention to unique learning styles, gifts, and strengths and what *energizes* each of us. Nathan has been a master at journeying into self-awareness through learning stories and inner work. He writes about his own self-awareness:

> *Today, I had a quick meeting with a guy from a private equity firm. On my way up the elevator, I was thinking about how I could make a good impression on him because I am attracted to working in private equity. Then I thought, "What if I do impress him? What if I end up getting a job here? Will that change my enjoyment of life?" My answer was no. I'd feel better about myself for having a sweet job, but I'd be thinking even more about how to succeed in a very competitive environment.*
>
> *The point? I do so much to make myself feel good about myself or to avoid my fear. Yet the "feel good" is always temporary, and fear is always worse than the realization of my fears. It doesn't make much sense to spend so much time with it.*
>
> *As I become more aware of what builds my ego, I can take my ego less seriously. As I take myself less seriously, my mind stops thinking so much. As my mind slows down, I'm more present. As I am more present, I notice things around and within me more. As I notice more, I feel myself and the things around me more. As I feel more, I start noticing the essence within me. As I notice my essence, I begin to see the connection between me and all and everything.*

Early on, I realized that our coaching medium would be Nathan's gift of story writing. He would have an enriching or troubling experience, and then he would write an essay about it. He would send me the essay, and we would talk about the meaning. After starting a new position at work and becoming frustrated at a wasteful situation, he wrote an essay that we titled

"Chipotle Anger." He was given an assignment that in reality required only three hours of work, but he was to be "available" for forty-six hours, including weekends and after-hours. Meaningless time wasted—but billable. We had great conversations about the misuse of talented people, the corporate values that would encourage this waste of resources, and the transformation we have to make inside ourselves to accept situations we don't have the authority to change. The subtitle for the essay became "Caution: If your people feel small, they will do small work."

> **"If your people feel small, they will do small work."**

There are countless articles and statistics on what millennials want in the workplace. And while there is truth to what is reported—e.g., wanting to be their own boss, more flexible work schedules, a desire to make the world a better place, etc.—Nathan continues to coach me that it is about more than that.

*Often, work feels like jail. I get that work is a choice, but it doesn't always feel like a choice. In all honesty, I don't want to ever work. I want to develop, create, write, analyze, communicate, consider, etc. . . . not work. For me, the solution to not working is understanding how my grunt work fits into the big picture.*

*For you [Duane], the solution is sacrificing the certain for the uncertain. Also, you're clear about what you want to do. You want to bring out the best in young people. However, you're uncertain about how to proceed. Young people don't have money, so they can't pay you. Well, you know what I say to that? Corporations do! The turnover rate at companies is unreal, and they don't know what to do about it. Money, titles, 401(k)s, opportunity, clear promotion schedules, etc., don't encourage or motivate my generation. There is a huge opportunity to teach corporations how to incentivize and retain young professionals. Do it! Please, for all the miserable young professionals jumping jobs every one and a half years.*

Nathan and I come from different experiences, but we continue to learn from each other. He is twenty-seven and living internationally in the first part of his career. I am fifty-nine and have never lived in another country. But he is right in his coaching to me. Uncertainty breeds fear in my Baby Boomer generation. We are heavily influenced by a history of market downturns, unemployment, and not being able to make mortgage payments. Millennials, on the other hand, have their own fear: FOMO (Fear of Missing Out). Researchers tell us that with so many choices today, there is a greater struggle with decision fatigue and constant second guessing ("What if I miss out on something better tomorrow by choosing *this* now?"). Enter *The Art of Coaching for Servant Leadership*, where we are taught to listen deeply, ask each other good questions, and learn from the genius in each other.

| Deborah Welch

## RELATIONAL BONDS ACROSS GENERATIONS

Duane and Nathan inspire me to look at gifts across generations more closely. I am touched by how they have explored their fears, differing gifts, and common values. I ask myself if there is any way I might reach out across generations as a servant-leader coach? Here is a second story about Duane, this time told by Ann, involving our choice in how we see our differences in relationships.

| Ann McGee-Cooper

## STRENGTH THROUGH DIFFERENCE

I frequently experience strength through difference with my business Partner, Duane Trammell. His primary responsibility is to manage the operations and financial health of our Company. My primary role is business development, taking responsibility to develop robust relationships with our Clients and keep us pushing the envelope in all our services and products.

Duane keeps us safe. I keep us pushing the edge. I often get energized about some research opportunity that will generate no revenue but may help many people and provide a great opportunity to practice and test some of our most innovative concepts. Can we afford the time and resources invested in my pilot projects? This is often a great opportunity for strength through difference. We have learned to listen with open minds and hearts to two very different ways of deciding where and how to invest our time, energy, and resources. Sometimes I pull back when I realize what won't get done if I push forward with my enthusiasm for new pilots. And sometimes Duane listens thoughtfully, and we find a third right answer, which means a way to combine the best of both ideas so that we both get more than we had anticipated. Over the years, we have discovered that much, if not most, of the not-for-profit work we have pioneered somehow attracts new Clients, new services, and new opportunities for revenue. We both realize that without our very different gifts and interests, these highly creative new ventures would never have happened, and our Company would never have benefited from the critical balance of fiscal stewardship versus creative innovation.

| Ann McGee-Cooper

## ASSUMING GOODWILL

Assuming goodwill is another foundation of servant leadership. We learn to respect differences and not fear them. For example, my beloved business Partner, Duane Trammell, doesn't like surprises or risks. His strengths are planning ahead in detail and making sure he has thought through each possibility. I, on the other hand, love spontaneity, challenge, and risk. I can feel bored and limited by too much planning and detail. I thrive on the unknown and enjoy the challenge of what seems to be impossible. My love for adventure and challenge ages my Partner with anxiety.

> **We learn to respect differences and not fear them."**

What we both have learned is that our extreme differences are balanced by leveraging our individual gifts. When we honor both his need to be fully prepared and eliminate all possible surprises and equally honor my appetite for the unknown, we perform at our collaborative best. Before I learned this truth, I used to place Duane in such stressful positions that he was operating at a deficit, and so was I because I had lost his best possible self (and seamless support!). Instead of assuming that he is obsessive and lacking courage, I have learned to appreciate that his gift is in seeing how unaddressed details can hold us prisoner. His brain sees these speed bumps whereas mine glosses over them. And instead of viewing me as an out-of-control dreamer, he chooses to honor my gifts for daring to believe that the impossible is only possible for those with the courage to persevere. By each assuming goodwill for the other, we harvest the best of our opposite and complementary strengths.

| Deborah Welch

## GROWING STRONG BONDS THROUGH ASSUMING GOODWILL

Ann's illustration speaks to the possibility that we can develop a strong fabric in relationships that can support greatness and giftedness. One key to working with an approach that finds strengths in differences is this attitudinal lens Ann describes when she suggests choosing to assume goodwill. Relationship patterns grow over time and become reinforced; it is very easy to put people into boxes or stereotype those whose strengths are different from our own. Once our habitual thinking patterns develop toward a Partner, it takes some concentrated effort to embrace a different perspective. Ann addresses this so powerfully when she says, "I used to place Duane in such stressful positions that he was operating at a deficit, and so was I because I had lost his best possible self." To foster her understanding and support of Duane's strengths, she reveals her own false assumptions. She shifts her attitude from judgment to goodwill. This raises a question we can ask ourselves as coaches: is there a subtle way in which we have become a part of the problem or at least less effective than we could be as coaches?

The core idea of assuming goodwill as a coach is worth reflecting on. The challenge this brings deserves some unpacking. It sounds so simple, but the more I reflect on it, the more I see opportunities to be generous in my view, more willing to assume goodwill.

Greenleaf said, "All that is needed is for enough servant-leaders to show the way, not by mass movements, but by each servant-leader demonstrating his or her unlimited liability for a specific group."[22] Perhaps we have experienced something like "unlimited liability" from a great mentor or a significant family member who believed in us more than we believed in ourselves, who took a risk for us or saw our best self at a time we couldn't. We can use coaching practices that encourage us to have more open views, but even our practices can become rigid. If that happens we need to understand the importance of opening our minds and our hearts.

Ann tells another story about a time it would have been easy to be offended or irritated, yet by staying peaceful and curious something powerful happened in her experience as a coach.

| Ann McGee-Cooper

## USING DISCOVERY QUESTIONS CAN TAKE COURAGE

Two very large corporations merged. One company bought the other, and the result was huge, polarizing judgments between them, creating a gulf of animosity. Neither corporation had anything good to say about the other. Our consulting team was brought in by one side of the fence to teach skills of high-performance teaming in a seminar format and follow up with monthly executive coaching. On one particular occasion, I had a coaching appointment with the chief operating officer (COO) from the other side of the fence. I was scheduled for a one-hour coaching session to help him find successful ways to apply the whole-brain leadership skills he was learning to his current challenges. We shook hands and I asked how could I provide the best possible support. In response, he was purposefully rude, saying, "Get out of my office." My response was, "I'll be glad to do that. But first may I ask for more information, so I understand where you are? Is it a lack of value from me and what we are teaching, or is it urgency with other things?"

Maybe it was both. But he began to describe a really ugly business challenge that was troubling him deeply. He needed to get on their corporate jet to travel from California to Australia to meet with the prime minister, and he didn't expect the meeting to come out well.

I responded, "I will gladly give you back this hour, no questions asked. But possibly I can help you. If you're flying that far and you're not sure that good things are going to come from it, maybe I can help you if you're open to telling me a little bit more." So he began to tell me the story of how at a cocktail party he had bullied his Client into this meeting. And he said, "What I can expect is I may fly all that way and he won't keep the appointment.

That would be a good way to rub my nose in it." As he told me more, he said this Client was suing his company for twenty million dollars. "So are you guilty?" I asked. He replied, "Yes, but we're fighting it. It's costing us approximately two hundred thousand dollars per month for our team of lawyers." And with another twenty million dollars at risk, obviously they didn't want to lose the suit. So he explained, "We just don't have much going for us because we didn't perform in the way we should have. And that will work against us. Also, we entered into the contract with the previous person in office who represents the opposing political party. This politician has an advantage because his lawyers are government lawyers costing him nothing. Our lawyers cost us. And at every opportunity, he goes to the media to say he's the hero because he's rubbing the Yanks' nose in it!"

So it really was kind of a no-win situation. Then a creative leap came to me. "What if you called ahead? You've got twenty-one hours of flight time. What if you apologized and admitted your rudeness—how you publically bullied him into granting this appointment—and acknowledge that he has every right not to meet with you. However, mention that you've been doing your homework and have a very interesting offer you'd like to make in person. Then on your flight down, with help from your staff, study the promises in his political platform to see if there's something else you can do with the two hundred thousand dollars you're spending every month for lawyers. Find out if you can put your company to work to solve problems that would make him a good guy in the eyes of the people that have elected him." An interesting side note is that our Client had a huge department of world-class petroleum engineers just sitting idle, waiting for the market to turn. Petroleum engineers are, in essence, very gifted problem solvers. My Client couldn't afford to furlough them because once the market turned they would be in high demand. But for now they were marking time. His company was already paying their salaries and here was an opportunity to put them to work literally turning a problem into an opportunity, with the added goal of winning back the trust of this Client by performing impressive value-added work!

> ❝A Client must believe there is value in the coaching to be open to the benefit.❞

When we started the session, the COO was sarcastic and not open to coaching on this challenge. But as I helped him begin to see other possibilities that made sense and potentially would have a successful business outcome, he became more interested. A Client must believe there is value in the coaching to be open to the benefit. As he listened and started to see the potential benefit, he began participating more in the conversation and sharing in the plan.

> **"How can the problem become an opportunity? Where can you use your gifts and work from what lights you up?"**

*The end of the story?* He succeeded in having the meeting. He called me immediately on the flight back to his home office in the U.S. and said, "We've got an agreement!" And that meant the twenty million dollars was no longer at risk. His staff had identified not only the political promises made by the prime minister but also several construction problems in aging government buildings that the company's engineers could easily address. The COO went into the meeting with a proposal to do asbestos abatement and replace slow elevators, plus other building upgrades, at no additional cost to this Client in return for dropping the lawsuit.

The problem became a huge opportunity and, in essence, in less than an hour coaching session together, we saved well over twenty million dollars. Also, over the course of the next year, we won back the loyalty of this Client, and future work was awarded thanks to this creative negotiation. I want to be quick to give generous credit to this Client. If he hadn't had the open-mindedness to listen, plus the willingness to be humble and trustworthy, this would have been only an interesting idea. It was his personal ability to sell the concept first to his Client and next to his team of petroleum engineers-turned-ambassadors to win back trust that helped them cross the finish line.

The lesson I would hope others would take from this is to park your fear and listen with an open mind and heart. If you err, own it. Just apologize and learn from it. Learn to face problems because problems are an opportunity for you to prove your worth and bring value. You can do that no matter what your gifts are.

As a coach, when Clients are stuck in challenges, ask the question, "How can the problem become an opportunity? In this situation, where can you use your gifts and work from what lights you up?" Ask open-ended questions to help your Client discover alternatives. How can their relationships and networks be used to create something better?

| Deborah Welch

## ASKING GOOD QUESTIONS AS A SERVANT-LEADER COACH

Take a moment to reflect on what Ann's story says for you. She shows a tremendous commitment to her own purpose to be truly helpful and serve, even when the person she is coaching is coming across in an offensive way. Ann attends to this relationship with a capacity to park fear and stay open to seek opportunity, even in times when a relationship might feel rough and strained. As an exceptional servant-leader coach, Ann asked great questions, found a way to use her gifts, and she acknowledged her Client for his open-mindedness and his efforts with his team to win back trust. A distinguishing feature of servant leadership coaching is seen in the way Ann brings her servant's heart into the relationship. The questions she asked demonstrated that. Ann's question, "How can the problem become an opportunity?" is based in wonder and humility. Edgar Schein wrote about humble inquiry, saying what is most important is to ask yourself about your motives before asking a question. He says, "Am I feeling humble and curious or have I fallen into thinking I have an answer and am I just testing out whether or not I am right?"[23] Testing a thought is not true open inquiry.

Fear and defensiveness can lead us to shut down on our Partners. When I notice myself having a negative attitude toward someone, I find that the use of humble, open inquiry can help me. Otherwise, my own perceptions may collude in my Partner's problem. Sometimes I reach out to a peer or coach to help me see a new perspective if I find that I am stuck in my own ideas and too deeply entrenched to ask an open question.

Jenny Inge told a story in one of our Virtual Servant Leadership Learning Community® circles that speaks to another way to open up to our Partners.

## MOVING FROM FRUSTRATION TO FASCINATION: A MIRROR FOR THE COACH | Jenny Inge

SINCE THE SEVENTIES, the concept of mirrors and metaphors in relationships, experiences, and even dreams has guided how I engage with life and keep myself ever growing. No practice or therapy has brought this to light better than my studies of Parelli Natural Horsemanship, which taught me that horsemanship does not mean owning a horse and making it perform for you—rather, it's a relationship, a partnership. And the human's role in this partnership is leadership. The tenets of this style of horsemanship actually mirror the universal principles of great leadership:

- Your horse doesn't care how much you know until he knows how much you care.

- Reward the slightest try—expect a lot, accept a little, and reward often.

- Be clear, consistent, fair, and firm without getting mad or mean.

- Never let your goals get in front of your principles.

- Make no assumptions.

- You cannot expect your horse to be physically, mentally, and emotionally fit unless you are physically, mentally, and emotionally fit first.

- Look where you want to go.

- Take the time it takes.

- Smile!

One of the ways these tenets reflect servant leadership is in the way they use "mirrors." Mirrors reveal to us something about ourselves that may have been hidden. I find that many mirrors show up when I'm playing and working with my horses—some of them painful. When I am focused on accomplishing a goal, task, or trick, I often fail to notice that I am bringing to the pasture frustrations and exhaustion from my day at work. I project those anxieties onto the horses, and I unexpectedly find them reflected back to me in the form of resistance and disrespect. If I react with frustration, the situation only gets worse. But as I relax into play, instead of work, things shift quickly and in a big way. I become curious rather than critical about their behavior, thinking out loud to myself, "Isn't it fascinating that ...?" As I soften, watch, and listen, the horses become more connected, engaged, and responsive. I never return from the pasture without learning something about them, myself, and others.

Frustration is fear—fear we will fail, that things won't go the way we want, that we will make a mistake or lose face. Fascination, on the other hand, is curiosity, confidence, empathy, and trust, open to infinite possibilities. As I begin to move from frustration to fascination—to become more present, focused, curious, and clear—my horses and I "magically" begin to accomplish things together as partners. Tears streaming down my face, grinning from ear to ear, I am filled with a wide range of emotions.

I am ashamed to recognize in my four-legged mirrors how often I sabotage relationships or the outcome of activities by over-managing; judging; being unclear, impatient, or unfair; or not rewarding or celebrating enough. At the same time, I am in awe of the infinite ways in which the universe teaches us. I feel restored and overjoyed to be reminded once again how easy life can be when we use our mirrors to help us let go of fear and live in trust.

| Deborah Welch

## MOVING FROM FRUSTRATION TO FASCINATION

Jenny speaks so beautifully to how we learn in relationships and how we can find mirrors to help us see more clearly. Also, she models this spirit of open questions, which are vital to great servant leadership coaching. For example, Jenny asks a provoking question, "How can I move from frustration to fascination?" Cynthia Watson adds some further insights to these points from Jenny.

## SELF-AWARENESS IS CENTRAL TO THE
## PRACTICE OF SERVANT LEADERSHIP COACHING | Cynthia Watson

I LOVE THE CONCEPT OF "ASSUMING GOODWILL." Stephen Covey's story of the cookie thief has stuck with me for many years.[24] It basically involves an individual who sits down at the airport with a bag of cookies. He is seated next to another individual. After a few minutes, he reaches into the bag of cookies that he set beside him and takes a cookie. He notices that the person next to him looks at him a little funny. But they smile and nod at each other. A few minutes later, the second individual reaches down and takes a cookie from the bag. The man who took the first cookie begins to get irritated and think to himself, "The nerve of this guy—eating *my* cookies without even asking permission!" They both take a second cookie, and the first individual continues to become more and more irate. Then he looks down and realizes that he is not eating from his bag of cookies but rather from the bag of cookies belonging to the person that he sat down beside!

There are times when I have come to realize that I may be "eating from someone else's cookie bag" after I've learned all the facts or I've gotten to a point that I can look at a situation differently. Sometimes I will take a quick time-out to remind myself that "all are doing the best they can." I have truly come to believe the truth in this statement, and it immediately shifts my thinking to a more compassionate place. It doesn't excuse inappropriate behaviors, because we all have to take responsibility for our actions and our decisions, but it helps me to view the person in the situation more compassionately and to keep my heart open in the situation. I've also come to value the question, "How can I see this situation differently?" and to remind myself that I can see things differently if I choose.

Seeing things differently requires me to look at the story that I am telling myself about people's motives, what they are thinking, their situation, etc. Frequently that story is just a projection of my mind telling me that someone else has her hand in my cookie bag.

I have had several occasions when I opened a dialogue with another person only to find that none of the things that I thought I "knew" were true. I love the Greenleaf quote that all that is needed is "each servant-leader demonstrating his or her unlimited liability for a specific group." It has always been my habit to keep words of inspiration near me in my office to reflect on throughout the day. One of the quotes on my desk that I find motivating is from Mother Teresa. She said something very similar to Greenleaf: "We can do no great things, only small things with

> **"We can do no great things, only small things with great love."**

great love."[25] The reason I find this so inspiring is that each of us has the ability to do small things regardless of our situation; it is overwhelming if we pressure ourselves into trying to do "great" things. Sometimes I find that what seem like "small" things to me may require great courage from another person and vice versa, depending upon our respective areas of giftedness. What sometimes gets in the way of assuming goodwill is usually my limited ability to move beyond my own ego.

I think that the relationship with one's self is the bedrock of all of our relationships. I have to be open and willing to hear feedback and to do the work necessary to grow into more self-awareness. Without self-awareness, I won't be aware of "when I have my hand in someone's cookie bag" or "when I am assuming goodwill." These are words that are easily said but not always easily practiced.

I have found that my ability to learn and grow through relationships is directly proportionate to my self-growth. To me, this means that I have to accept my personal responsibility to keep my own bucket filled and be willing to do the work to grow and expand. One mirrors the other. The more I grow in self-awareness, the more that I expand my ability to practice strength through difference, assuming goodwill, parking fear, and going from frustration to fascination. Isn't that part of the point behind Jenny's illustrations of the horses? As she became quiet and expanded her self-awareness, she began to see into that mirror. It's an upward spiral.

When I was playing tennis, I frequently had the same experience with my tennis that Jenny had with the horses. In fact, I used to jokingly say that whatever I was dealing with in life would show up on the tennis court. If I was experiencing fear and self-doubt, then invariably I would become nervous and fearful of taking my shots. If my expectations of myself were too high, then I would become frustrated. Often I was so busy in my day-to-day life that I was out of touch with what was actually going on inside, but it became pretty apparent on the tennis court. Once I discovered this truth, I began to work on my "inner game" before I ever stepped on the court. I also learned that I could shift the energy in a tennis match by catching my internal dialogue and changing it. I remember one day when I was becoming increasingly frustrated with myself and my game, I made a conscious effort to shift my inner thoughts to practice gratitude. I would consciously look at my opponents and think of them as my teachers—they were teaching me to play at a higher level. I began thinking that I was grateful that they were playing with me. I thought about what a beautiful day it was and how fortunate I was to be healthy and active. Once I shifted my thinking and began looking for opportunities to express gratitude, my entire perspective and my game changed. What started as a frustration became a joy—which I think supports Jenny's illustration of turning frustration into fascination.

| Deborah Welch

## RECOGNIZING DIGNITY AND SPIRIT AS A SERVANT-LEADER COACH

Cynthia's point about choosing to turn from frustration toward a spirit of gratitude marks a choice to turn inward to grow. I love her observation that "my ability to learn and grow through relationships is directly proportionate to my self-growth." This movement toward self-growth is at the heart of servant leadership coaching. This requires dignity and respect for our coaching Partner and for ourselves.

**"My ability to learn and grow through relationships is directly proportionate to my self-growth."**

## REFLECTIONS

In the "Coaching with a Servant's Heart" chart in appendix A, you will find ideas that correspond to this chapter. Also, the questions below are designed to explore how to take your own coaching work further:

**1** *Have I considered using an assessment to map out the gifts and strengths in a partnership or team?*

**2** *How can I better respect differences with someone I am coaching and use "strength through difference" to build more trusting relationships?*

**3** *Has someone assumed goodwill, given me the benefit of the doubt, or taken a risk believing in me? What happened and how did that affect me? Is there a person or situation that comes to mind in which I could assume more goodwill today?*

**4** *What helps me ask questions and stay curious when I get locked into an old pattern of seeing things when I am leading or coaching?*

**5** *How willing am I to park my fears, keep my heart open, and stay curious in difficult moments?*

**6** *Once Ann and the COO found a sense of shared purpose, something powerful happened. How can I remind myself to keep a shared purpose at the center of my coaching work?*

# USING INQUIRY AND SILENCE TO MOVE BEYOND INTERFERENCE

WHAT GETS IN THE WAY
of our growth toward greatest
use of strengths? Developing
understanding of our areas of
weakness or our blind spots
opens the door to greater

self-awareness. In this chapter, we will consider the many challenges to using our gifts and strengths. Some of these include lack of self-awareness, overusing or misusing our strengths, and the tendency to disown our strengths or neglect giving time and focus to unfolding our unique talents in ways that work in relationships with others.

*We will explore four key possibilities for working with interference:*

1. *How we can help individuals understand their own inner resistance to growth*

2. *How strengths get overused or misused, and ways to grow self-awareness and learn signals to help adjust our use of strengths*

3. *Questions coaches can ask of ourselves or the leaders we are coaching to get through interference*

4. *How silence can be useful in a coaching process*

❝Our strengths are the source of our best contributions, our best thinking, and our best overall work. But there are also negative qualities that can emerge from each strength called *shadows*. Shadow is anything that we don't see or that we may dislike in ourselves."

| Deborah Welch

## MISUSING OUR STRENGTHS

Duane Trammell says, "Our strengths are the source of our best contributions, our best thinking, and our best overall work. But there are also some negative qualities that can emerge from each strength, qualities of thinking that are not productive. We call these negative qualities shadows. *Shadow* is anything that we as leaders don't see or that we may dislike in ourselves. This can stifle a partnership's potential."[26]

> **Once we are aware of the shadow side of our greatest strengths, it is possible to avoid getting blindsided."**

Every year in our Virtual Servant Leadership Learning Community (VSLLC®) we take time to consider leadership shadow. We ask ourselves, "Is there a way that one of my strengths turns to shadow when I am under stress or overly passionate?"

Sometimes it is simple. For example, someone in a servant leadership learning circle will say, "Public speaking is a strength of mine, but I talk too much, and if I am not careful I can walk right over people." Or, "I am an analytical engineer, and understanding how things work is my greatest strength. But last week when an airplane was making a loud noise just outside our home, I spent too much time telling [my wife] the logic and science around it. The more I explained the science the worse she felt. I had to become aware that my strength was flipping into shadow."

Here is another example. Looking at her belief strength on a strengths assessment, someone noted, "This strength helps me to pour encouragement into the young people I serve in a way that I hope will go with them for the rest of their lives ... But that same belief strength gets in my way if I am too rigid. I remember a time I held so strongly to my own belief, whether it was right or wrong, just so someone would know he could not push me over. I told him 'as long as Advil is produced we could go head-to-head all day long.' Now I understand that I was misusing this strength. I will help others in my organization to ensure their talents are better used in ways that work and are not compromised."

Ann McGee-Cooper often says, "Our weaknesses are our strengths worn inside out." We frequently are blind to the Achilles heel side of our strengths. In our VSLLC® program, we review an article which helps us see the shadow side of four categories of strengths as measured by an assessment called the *Herrmann Brain Dominance Instrument*®.[27] It shows us how a strength in developing structures can cause us to be too rigid, for strong attention to detail can result in being too detailed. A wonderful speaking ability can result in being overly talkative, and the ability to see the whole picture and dream big can lead us to become too impatient or seem to be dreaming more than doing.

Once we are aware of the shadow side of our greatest strengths, it is possible to avoid getting blindsided, especially if we find a learning Partner who calls us back when we are out of balance or not in harmony. We can ask, "Can you cue me when I need to step back and allow other's strengths to be heard and used?" Many servant-leaders will hone in on one area for self-development and ask their entire team for help.

| Deborah Welch

## DISOWNING OUR SPECIAL GIFTS

Sometimes we think that serving others means that we lift everyone else up and ignore our own talents. It is crucial to understand that true humility involves attending to your own gifts with the same care you would give to someone else's. It is one thing to recognize that we need to "put the oxygen mask on ourselves before reaching out to help others." It is another thing to actually make a change in ourselves toward more courageously caring for our own gifts and staying on course to grow our capacities.

In an earlier chapter, Ann described a point in her life when she focused on serving only her husband's strengths and ignored her own. I asked her to recount a moment when she went from just focusing on bringing out the genius in others to looking for her own strengths and genius. She explained that recognizing her own genius has emerged in many layers throughout her life. Here is one memorable time when she was helping teachers to teach gifted children.

| Ann McGee-Cooper

## ATTENTION TO UNIQUENESS IN SERVANT LEADERSHIP

If we celebrate our own genius, we can be quickly marked as arrogant or over confident. When I was leading a teacher education program for gifted children, I realized that it felt safe to say to these children, "Oh, you are so gifted!" But that in itself doesn't really help them because most of us are criticized when we express our genius. We can start to feel like a target. Or, once we reveal our unique genius, we are then held to a higher standard and criticized when we don't do everything perfectly. What these gifted kids needed to see was a role model, someone who is living their gifts with all the courage that takes. I needed to reach within myself to model living up to my own potential so I could help other teachers learn to model living their gifts. I designed a curriculum called "Awakening Sleeping Genius"[28] and said to the teachers, "This whole semester will be about living your genius. We are not going to judge your genius. We are on a journey to find out more about it. What is it like? This is not about how good you are; this is about exploring what it is like to discover your own genius and having the courage to live it. It takes a leap of faith." It was mind-blowing to see what happened that year for the teachers and the children.

To grow as a servant-leader you must dare to believe, have the courage to identify your strengths … and then invite these special gifts to unfold in all aspects of your life. This is important work in servant leadership. When I learned to give my own gifts more space in my life, it allowed me to serve others more effectively. I felt so unprepared to do the work Greenleaf asked me to do in those early years. He just smiled and said, "Create dangerously … Trust yourself and you'll know. Never doubt your gifts, only doubt your ability to give them space in your life."

> "Create dangerously… Trust yourself and you'll know. Never doubt your gifts, only your ability to give them space in your life."

Greenleaf continually affirmed my uniqueness. He was a master at asking open questions. He would ask me questions and was truly curious about my answers. I learned quickly that he didn't expect me to answer right away; he was posing something for me to ponder. He would smile at me and say, "Live with the question." He was prompting me to take my thinking to a different level. It was one of many ways he encouraged me to listen to and trust my intuition and my genius.

| Deborah Welch

## PURSUING GREATER POTENTIAL

The focus on realizing greater potential for both leaders and coaches is evident in Ann's story. This kind of encouragement is often easier for us to provide for others than for ourselves. Pursuing our greater potential can feel antithetical to servant leadership. Most servant-leaders grasp the meaning and joy in serving others. It is paradoxical that we derive our greatest joy from serving others and so often get much more in return than we give. But many of us hold ourselves back. We can ignore our own gifts or leave them in the margins of our lives. Robert Greenleaf described how he sought to cultivate "entheos," or being lit up from within. He added, "Awareness is not always a giver of solace, but great leaders have an inner serenity." He urged us, "Think of yourself as a person with unique potentialities" because a central purpose in life is that we "bring these potentialities into full bloom."[29]

Matt Kosec has a bold way of explaining what this takes.

### LIVING OUR GIFTS | Matt Kosec

"ALL THAT IS NEEDED TO REBUILD COMMUNITY as a viable life form for large numbers of people," states Greenleaf, "is for enough servant-leaders to show the way, not by mass movements, but by each servant-leader demonstrating his or her own unlimited liability for a quite specific community-related group."[30] Greenleaf wrote this while discussing the shift from business-as-institution to business-as-community.

Here, Greenleaf reminds us that servant leadership starts from within. "Unlimited liability" can include many aspects, but certainly one of them is the willingness to accept our own imperfections and those instances when we've given less than our very best. The best of us, though, have a coach or mentor who is willing to show care and compassion by reminding us when we are not giving our very best. Authentic feedback, combined with our humility, allows us to grow closer toward servant leadership.

Starting within, however, brings the ethical imperative to live into all of our gifts. Ann McGee-Cooper has often reminded us that we shelter our "genius," that particular part of us that is our very best that we can bring into community. We hide it because of organizational experiences that make our genius seem intolerably different from the status quo. Or perhaps it cannot shine because of so many organizational rules and structures—well intended but a poor substitute for community expectations and covenants that truly hold us accountable to each other.

The challenge, then, is to live into our genius, our gifts, as though it is a moral imperative and an obligation to the organizational community. Could you imagine the organization that could be built if everyone felt comfortable displaying their genius?

| Deborah Welch

## ADJUSTING OUR USE OF STRENGTHS

Many of us have had these "organizational experiences that make our genius seem intolerably different from the status quo." I don't know anyone who hasn't felt at some time the giving up of a part of oneself either during school or in an early workplace environment. Often this is because our gifts are misunderstood. Rules, structures, and conventions don't fit with our uniqueness.

As Sir Ken Robinson puts it in one of the most highly watched TED Talks:

*I meet all kinds of people who don't enjoy what they do. They simply go through their lives getting on with it. They get no great pleasure from what they do. They endure it rather than enjoy it and wait for the weekend. But I also meet people who love what they do and couldn't imagine doing anything else. If you said to them, "Don't do this anymore," they'd wonder what you were talking about. Because it isn't what they do, it's who they are. They say, "But this is me, you know. It would be foolish for me to abandon this because it speaks to my most authentic self." And it's not true of enough people. In fact, on the contrary, I think it's still true of a minority of people. I think there are many possible explanations for it. And high among them is education because education, in a way, dislocates very many people from their natural talents. And human resources are like natural resources; they're often buried deep. You have to go looking for them; they're not just lying around on the surface. You have to create the circumstances where they show themselves.*[31]

Life's difficult events and dysfunctional patterns can cause us to lose sight of the fundamental truth of who we are and what we have to give. As servant leadership coaches, we can help our Partners learn to discover strengths that have been pushed on the margins or gone unused. There are many ways we can go looking for strengths or adjust their use.

| Deborah Welch

## ASKING THE QUESTION, "CAN I ADD MORE COMPASSION?"

We over-focus on problems or areas that are not where our greatest gifts reside. Several fellow servant-leaders and I had a wonderful conversation on weaknesses with Duane and Ann. Duane said that weaknesses might simply stem from preferences that we have. If we like to work with emotions, we may not enjoy facts and figures, and thus we become weaker in math. "What we don't prefer, we don't do as much, and like muscles in the body, this attribute slides into a weakness." Yet we often keep pushing ourselves to fit into someone else's style of leading. We try to be the great speaker our mentor is when our gift is facilitation. Or we try to be more "well-rounded." Research shows that one of the best things we can do about an area where we are lacking is team

> **"...one of the best things we can do about an area where we are lacking is team with others who have opposite yet complementary strengths."**

with others who have opposite yet complementary strengths. Yet the old "lone hero" mentality leads us to try to be all things to all people.

Weaknesses can be blown out of proportion in organizations because there is a strong deficit focus. An over-focus on what is missing, an over-focus on deficits or weaknesses, often leads to a lack of compassion for ourselves. We just need to make a mental note and shift gears when we notice our own cynicism or lack of energy for something. It benefits us to partner with someone who has a complementary strength in order to reach a goal.

The important thing is that you explore your shadow side instead of seeing it from a negative perspective. An aspect of the shadow side for us is to be too harsh rather than to be invitational with ourselves and others. The predominant situation in the majority of organizations is still a deficit kind of thinking, with over-focus on problems. Cynicism often is rooted in what researchers call "negativity bias."[32] Many of us have been trained to dwell in negatives and to over-focus on our areas of weakness. When working with strengths and genius, we make a shift away from deficit focus. We don't ignore weaknesses, failures, or flaws; we learn to use our strengths to address them. We realize we may sometimes overuse our strengths, but we learn to be less self-critical and more responsible, continually striving to change. A good question we can ask our Partners and ourselves is, "Am I being compassionate?"

Ann tells this story in which she utilizes neuroscience when coaching.

| Ann McGee-Cooper

## NEURAL HIJACKING

I was coaching a very traditional, top-down, command-and-control leader who was exceedingly bright and creative and very quick to judge and criticize his direct reports. When I asked permission to explore this behavior with him and the unintended consequences, he lost interest quickly, telling me that at the salaries he paid these leaders, he could treat them any way he chose. I continued to ask questions about how he harshly intimidated them and then would remark about their mental incompetence. I kept asking questions to raise his awareness of the link between embarrassing someone about their intelligence and them becoming less sharp. Could this be the result of a neural hijacking that happens when we become afraid and 70 percent of blood leaves the brain and rushes into the muscles of the arms and legs to prepare for fight or flight? In this instant, adrenaline-induced response a person becomes very strong and very dumb ... which can be a dangerous combination.

| Deborah Welch

## COACHING QUESTIONS ABOUT UNINTENTIONAL CONSEQUENCES

In this very short story, Ann speaks volumes about how coaching questions can be used to help us consider the unintentional consequences of using sharp criticism or cruel words. Just as we can be too harsh with others, we can also be too harsh with ourselves. When I gain awareness that my strengths are misused or I get a picture of how I could improve, I can easily become impatient or overly critical with myself. This is antithetical to my growth.

Distinguishing how shadow work differs from the old deficit-based thinking is a little paradoxical. It has to do with the attitude with which we work with shadow; it is not the same as over-focusing on weakness or deficits. As servant leadership coaches, we expect to find genius even *in* the shadow. We learn to be nonjudgmental and curious toward whatever comes up. We just keep gravitating more toward strengths use, not forcing it but rather inviting it to reveal itself as our teacher and inviting our Partners to build the momentum in using their strengths as well. Adding humor and laughing at ourselves and our humanness helps those we are serving to do the same.

What interferes with our use of our gifts and strengths? The following story is a continuation of the interview with Dawna Markova.

## INTERFERENCE: WHAT GETS
## IN THE WAY OF OUR POTENTIAL | Dawna Markova

*Dawna:* There's a wonderful formula that I learned from Timothy Gallwey who wrote *The Inner Game of Tennis*,[33] and the formula is

$p = P - I$. As he described it, it's "p" (performance) equals P (Potential) – I (Interference). In essence, the people I work with want help learning how to minimize the interference. We create interference for ourselves, we create interference with others, and we create interference organizationally for people. We intuitively know in our guts, our heart, and our brain that the interference is there. It's like trying to tune in a radio station, but all you can hear is the static. The static we sense within and between us is interference to the highest state of energy, the lighting up that happens when we align our innate thinking talents with what really matters to us.

In a three-hour workshop I facilitated with the top two hundred leaders of GE Global Finance, people were being charged with shifting focus to become innovative leaders and thinkers. They were terrified! They had gotten to the top of the leadership ladder by thinking in ways that made the organization stable and secure. In order to think innovatively, you have to literally open your mind and go through chaos, which they were taught was the enemy. Often in the corporate world, the unknown is thought of as the devil itself. The two hundred people had no idea how to open their minds to the unknown and create possibilities. They had gotten to the top by thinking in very standardized, secure, rigid ways. They had forgotten long ago how to open their mind and navigate the unknown through innovative ways of thinking. I had to help them remember a time when they had thought like that; they literally had to recollect that potential they once had.

> **"To think innovatively, you literally have to open your mind and go through chaos."**

*Deborah:* What is that like as they move toward their potential?

*Dawna:* Right now in my life, I'm working with four thinking Partners. I'm writing a movie with my son. I'm finishing two books for Random House about collaborative intelligence and relational intelligence. And I'm seventy-three. My inner world is calling me also. I am shifting my awareness inward. Instead of risking my significance, I'm beginning to risk my insignificance. I'm devoting more and more of my time to silence, to a deeper listening, a slower rhythm. I'm needing to explore one question for thirty-six hours or three days if I need to.

Whether working with people or diving into solitude, there are four questions which are my life's compass points: "What's unfinished for me to give, to learn, to experience? How can I use the gifts and talents that I have to love the life I am living?"

We all have been educated for a world that no longer exists. Our handholds in the darkness are understanding what talents bring you more alive and what are the gifts that only you can bring to the rest of us. You have to know how to re-energize yourself. You have to understand the rhythm of your neurological system, which includes neural nets around your heart and intestines. We literally think with our brains, our hearts, and our guts. It's necessary therefore, to access and align all three so they collaborate with each other instead of interfere.

| Deborah Welch

## QUESTIONS TO GET THROUGH THE STATIC

Dawna reminds us that resistances and fears and anxiety will arise. Good discernment practices and the ability to ask significant questions can guide us through the static. We will get off track, but how we got off track is less important than having something we can hold onto through the day to help us get back more quickly when we lose clarity. Although we often may wish for less fog on this inner journey, we can learn to ask ourselves questions that orient us.

Dawna suggests starting the day off by asking a question that we can't answer. Some questions will help us gravitate toward our true self, our sense of purpose, and toward unearthing our gifts. Dawna illustrates by using the question, *"How can I accomplish the tasks in front of me today using my talents rather than a carrot and stick?"* This is a great question. I invite each of you to try it out first thing tomorrow morning.

Another question that I found from poet David Whyte is, "What is the elemental water which will help me live into my gifts today, and how can I move toward my natural element?" In his book *Crossing the Unknown Sea*, Whyte tells us about his own journey when he decided to become a professional poet, a field where few can make a living. There was little encouragement for him to follow this career path, and he had many obligations that made it challenging. But he reflects on a poem by Rainer

Rilke about a swan. In the poem, the swan looks awful as she waddles awkwardly over the ground. But once she is on the water, everything changes. The swan glides with ease and grace. He says we are like that awkward, waddling swan outside of the water, trying to push ourselves harder and beating ourselves up if we can't move faster. But the "swan doesn't cure her awkwardness by pushing harder, by saying 'When the going gets tough the tough get going.' The swan simply moves toward the water. . . . It is the simple contact with the water that gives her grace and presence."

Whyte says that during a time when he needed to make a transition in his own life, he asked himself, "What is my elemental water? What is my place of belonging?" This freed him to move into the field of poetry. He surrounded himself with the elements that allowed him to thrive, and then he simply looked at taking small steps toward his highest priorities. He took one action a day toward growing as a poet. He noted, "One thing a day became a powerful multiplier."

Whyte says we should ask ourselves, "What is the elemental water in which I can glide? What are clues to my place of belonging? What kind of support feels like entering elemental water, and what could bring me more balance and grace in my life?"[34] As a servant-leader coach, sometimes I find that I am working too hard at change. Working too hard to help someone else with a change he or she would like to make is a sure sign of my being off track when I am coaching. And if I work too hard, I find that I get in my own way, which is another kind of interference or static. Practices that access a deeper wisdom help me avoid the temptation to overwork. I can usually find a more efficient approach to any work if I slow down to access wisdom. This leads to a final story.

| Deborah Welch

## THE USE OF SILENCE BRINGS FORTH DEEPER WISDOM

The status quo most of the time in the workplace is "perform, perform, perform," with little time taken for capacity building or finding a rhythm in our work that helps us stay renewed rather than get burned out. There is always so much more that can be accomplished, and many of us feel a constant urgency. I love Ann's story of her meeting Robert Greenleaf with a list of questions, feeling a great urgency to get answers. The first thing he did when she arrived was to have her take time with him in silence.

Inviting time for silence can seem countercultural. Yet there is a growing body of research on contemplative practices, mindfulness practices, and the use of silence in leadership and in coaching. Otto Scharmer studied 150 top thinkers and practitioners of innovation and leadership and noted they practice something regularly that helps them "access their best source of creativity and self." He said, "Many rise early in order to use the silence of the early morning hours to connect to their own purpose or essential self. . . . Some people seek the silence of nature. Some people meditate . . . some exercise." He provides a full range of activities that "create for yourself a place of deep reflection and silence that helps you to connect with what is most essential for you."[35]

> "Practices that access a deeper wisdom help me avoid the temptation to overwork."

Similarly, Joseph Jaworski tells the story of David Marsing, a senior officer at Intel. After he suffered a near-fatal heart attack, he observed, "I always knew that Intel was a high-stress environment, but I'd thought of myself as somehow above it. . . . As he lay in the hospital bed and reflected on his true purpose, "to help people realize that they have more potential than they ever imagined they had," he made a conscious choice to go back into a stressful environment but to do it with a very different perspective. David introduced reflective or contemplative practices at alternating weekly staff meetings. He said, "At first people weren't sure if I was serious. Many doubted that it would last. But over time they found these very helpful in slowing down, being much more aware of their environment and opening up." Eventually, these new practices and David's new outlook led to one of Intel's biggest successes. Fab 11 went from startup to full-volume production in record time, allowing Intel to recoup its $2.5 billion investment not in several years, as expected, but in just five short months. In addition to his personal practices to find inner stillness, David explained that this time in staff meetings helped "people tap into their innate ability . . . We taught them the positive effect of slower brainwave states as a way to develop an awareness that leads to unique solutions."[36]

In another story, Joel Marquardt tells about using some of these methods when two production managers didn't seem to be aware of what was happening on the shop floor. After talking to them for weeks, he decided instead to ask them to experiment with walking around the factory floor once an hour just to observe. *The direct order was that they could do nothing—not try to move a person to another work station or solve problems.* Joel invited these leaders to slow down their internal noise, just notice, and then reflect together. This dramatically changed the way they decided to lead.[37] Slowing down to see anew can be powerful.

In his book *It's Not About the Coffee*, Howard Behar expresses the importance of silence and of getting out of all the noise when he says,

> *Workplaces are, ironically, full of noise. We've got the large egos of people trying to succeed and make a difference. We've got the noise in our heads—all those inner voices telling us how to be, what to do, and what not to do. . . . When your ego is clamoring, "Pay attention to me," you need to work hard to see it for what it is: noise. Wherever the big noise comes from, it can keep you from hearing the truth; it can keep you from hearing the substance of what's really going on and what really needs to be done. If you listen to the still small voice—in yourself, in the people you lead, in the Customers you serve, and in the Partners you work with—you'll stay close to your values and to what matters most to you and the rest of the organization. If you listen to that small voice, you will develop the habits of the servant-leader, the best leader of all.*[38]

> **"If you listen to that small voice, you will develop the habits of the servant-leader, the best leader of all."**

Howard's words suggest that we learn to discern, to listen to the still small voice, and yet rarely do we find classes in our universities or organizations helping us to learn this kind of thing. Something extraordinary happens when Partners say, "Let's slow down and access deeper wisdom in the way we work together." That leads to the following servant leadership coaching story.

Ginny Gilmore has always been an innovator. In her seventeen years with her family business, she used a relational sales and marketing approach with Customers. The business growth was exponential, and upon the sale of the business she was able to found Sophia Foundation to continue to teach and learn about leadership in ways that supported others in their strengths and possibilities. In 2007 she partnered with Christa Williams, who became executive director. They dedicated themselves to working together in a manner that would change the old, unconscious patterns they had previously experienced in the workplace. They wanted to truly "be the change" they hoped to see in the workplace and community. I have had the honor of working with them these past few years, and one of many lessons for me has been the power of working with Partners in coaching. Coaching in partnerships is an opportunity that can easily be missed. For example, when I first got involved with strengths work as a servant leadership coach, it was completely energizing for me and the leaders I was working with. But then, as I continued on that the path, I saw the barriers that crop up that contribute to strengths work being just a "quick fix that backfires." The real fruit of strengths work happens over time. A great deal of the learning occurs through relationships. Many change leaders move right from individual strengths assessment work to team activities, and work with teams is vital. But one thing that is underestimated is the power of finding a Partner who is dedicated to building a trusting relationship and is willing to slow down in order to practice a deeper kind of listening. This kind of partnering can be pivotal in bringing out our best selves, as the following dialogue with Ginny and Christa shows.

### BUILDING TRUSTING RELATIONSHIPS | Ginny Gilmore

MOST OF MY LEADERSHIP CAREER, I didn't have the help of servant leadership coaching. I never experienced the greatest capacity of connecting my own strengths with my Partner's strengths. I did not support some of my Partners in the best ways that I could have. As I look back, it is clear to me now that most of my career I have been an activator. I like to help things move quickly to action. Many times I would present a creative idea of mine that I was sure was wonderful, and I would be shocked to see that my Partner seemed unhappy, upset, or irritated. What I have learned to do through servant leadership coaching is to support my Partner, Christa, in a whole different way. We have learned when to slow things down. If one of us shuts down, we pause. In a coaching session, Deborah might ask us how we are feeling. We might take a moment of silence together or decide to sleep on a decision before making it.

We are doing highly innovative work, and there are times that it gets hard. Christa and I will look at each other and realize we had made a promise to develop caring community (Sophia's vision), but sometimes we have no idea how to proceed. We turn to coaching in the times that are challenging or fear-provoking. We find our way to more appreciative, energizing, and creative strategies for our partnering and for our organization.

## SLOWING DOWN TO CREATE ROOM FOR STRONG IDEAS | Christa Williams

IT DOESN'T JUST HAPPEN ONCE that we slow down and find a way to collaborate to bring out the best in each other's strengths; it's ongoing growth and learning and work and commitment and smiles and sometimes tears. For example, if I hear the feedback Ginny gives me as "you are doing this wrong," I can doubt myself or overwork or feel less confident. When I remember how much I trust Ginny and have experienced how she wants to bring my giftedness into the world, I will take some time away to reflect, and typically I can re-engage in positive ways. Inevitably, by slowing down and leaving room for new ideas, I realize something great that we can co-create together. I begin to see the comment that first shut me down in a completely different light. Coaching helps to heal that place in me and in our partnership that can shut down and limit our potential. Instead, coaching, silence, and reflection work together to open up our potential."

| Deborah Welch

## FINDING THE WAY TO GREATER CALM AND CREATIVITY

Work that is transformational involves unpredictability, risks, and courage. Looking at our blind spots and the shadow side of our strengths can feel risky. We can become self-critical and stop our progress. Finding the way to greater calm and creativity starts by lowering the noise level from outside ourselves and our own self-criticisms and taking time to listen for a quieter voice inside. As Albert Einstein said, "A quiet life stimulates the creative mind." When Ginny, Christa, and I quiet our minds during a coaching session, wiser and more innovative ideas emerge. As a servant-leader coach, I bring a moment of silence to the session. In the beginning of a coaching call, I might read a quote and ask for a moment of silence, or halfway through I might ask for a moment to journal on a question and then ponder in silence. A tranquil moment of companionable silence can deepen the conversation in amazing ways. It is not only helpful for my Partners; it's vital for me. The cacophony of monkey mind inside is stilled, making room for ourselves to just be—so that we allow to surface that which rarely has a chance to surface within us. It can feel like an atmospheric change and raise the standard of our thoughts.

> "A tranquil moment of companionable silence can deepen the conversation in amazing ways."

Inviting a moment of silence comes with risks in the beginning of a coaching relationship. As someone said recently, "When there's a silent lull, part of me is just waiting for the other person to say, 'If you're not going to talk, then I've got better things to do with my time than sit here.'" Yet in order to help my Partners access their own inner wisdom, I have learned that how I use silence is just as important as what I say when I am coaching. Sometimes nothing seems to happen in the silence. Other times, I am surprised and delighted by the insights that drop in.

When I leave a coaching session when there was not enough "air time," I can see how there was less innovation, less of the stillness when a Partner might notice how she had drifted away from what lights her up. Or there might be self-criticism instead of just noticing that a strength was overused. The effect of a tranquil atmosphere is best described in this poem by Judy Brown:

## *Fire*

What makes a fire burn
is space between the logs,
a breathing space.
… Too many logs
packed in too tight
can douse the flames …

When we are able to build
open spaces
in the same way
we have learned
to pile on the logs,
then we can come to see how …
We only need to lay a log
lightly from to time.

A fire
grows
simply because the space is there,
with openings
in which the flame
that knows just how it wants to burn
can find its way.[39]

Use of silence creates a space that can entice something to occur that is as natural as flames burning fully and brightly. It draws us to a deeper state of heart. As a servant-leader coach, try exploring how the use of silence is helpful, when it happens, what makes it challenging, and how these practices may grow. What I find lines right up with Otto Scharmer's suggestion, "Going forward, the development and refinement of practicing collective silence will prove to be one of the most important leverage points for future leadership work."[40]

As we finished our conversation, Christa expressed what this has meant to her:

*Learning to have reflective practices and silence has become something I value and rely on in doing my work with Ginny and certainly with others within Sophia and in the community. Through coaching, a greater and deeper wisdom emerges, we find creative ideas, and our work is magnificent in ways that help our community open its heart to its greater self.*

When I think of a community opening its heart to itself, I recall attending Sophia Foundation community events where you might enter a room with 150 to 200 individuals from all sectors—corporations, schools, government, law enforcement, hospice, abuse centers, and more. And all are greeting each other with warm smiles and hugs, choosing to learn together how to lead in better ways. When I talk to community members afterwards they express being more present in their work, more available and caring, and renewed in a way that they can be a greater asset to the community.

As Ginny and Christa continue learning to nurture their own spirits and bring their greatest strengths to their work with the board and the community, the organization meets its mission to "nurture the spirit, dignity and potential of all people." Or as Gary Boelhower wrote, "Sophia Foundation is on the growing edge of wisdom practices."[41] Working with Ginny and Christa over these years, I am reminded that we have phenomenal capacities we can access in our partnerships that can then extend out and support others.

| Deborah Welch

## NURTURING THE GREATER SELF

In the work of servant leadership coaching, there is a huge wellspring that can be tapped when you learn to embrace your strengths, but the road to get there has many twists and turns. In this chapter we considered many of the ways we may encounter interference and some ideas to help those we are coaching move beyond the static. Stories in this chapter illustrate the value of getting input from others, learning to ask ourselves good questions, and exploring our areas for growth with less harshness and more compassion.

**We have phenomenal capacities we can access in our partnerships that can then extend out and support others."**

## REFLECTIONS

In the "Coaching with a Servant's Heart" chart in appendix A, you will find ideas for application from this chapter. To apply guiding ideas, consider one of the questions for reflection below:

**1** *As a coach, what strengths do you tend to overdo under stress, and what are the signals it's time to adjust your use of your strengths?*

**2** *When static comes up and interferes with your high state of energy and use of gifts, how can you find your way through it?*

**3** *What guiding question could you ask yourself daily that might help you through interference as it arises?*

**4** *How can you help a Partner approach a shadow or weakness with more respect and curiosity and less fear or harshness?*

**5** *In addition to being on this journey working with strengths and genius in yourself, what is important in how you coach others?*

# THE CONTINUOUS APPROACH OF THE SERVANT LEADER COACH

IN THIS FINAL CHAPTER, we offer some coaching lessons and how best to put the essential elements of coaching for servant leadership into practice along with some tools to use. These tools are not meant to apply to all coaching situations, nor is this a comprehensive list.

*In this chapter, we will cover three main areas for practice:*

1.  *Practices to deepen respect (Give ownership of the process to the person being coached. Determine coachability, both for your Clients and for yourself. Are you willing to be a student? Reframe toxic language.)*

2.  *Practices to enhance learning (PLUS/DELTA and Ladder of Inference)*

3.  *Practices to enhance energy (celebration and appreciation)*

**❝I learned that it was critical for me to be the Clients' student and learn as much as possible about them, their lives, and challenges, both personal and professional."**

| Ann McGee-Cooper

## LESSONS LEARNED AS A SERVANT-LEADER COACH

In the eighties, my business Partner, Duane Trammell, and I were coaching teams of leaders in several business industries, teaching them servant leadership. We would plan in-depth, interactive one-day sessions with two months between the sessions for everyone to practice the new skills they were learning. But the intensity of people's schedules seemed to crowd out practice. As a result, we learned to check in with individuals by phone or in person for an hour to help them stay focused on their personal action plan (the commitments they made during the

> **❝Clients would tell me that one of the things they appreciated was my transparency about my own struggles and imperfections."**

session to practice new skills). Through this process, we learned how to make this experience more robust and sustainable. These ideas can be woven into coaching on an "as appropriate" basis.

First, I learned that it was critical for me to be the Clients' student and learn as much as possible about them, their lives, and challenges, both personal and professional.

By being their student, I could model asking good questions and honor them by entering into their world. When I use the term *honoring*, I mean putting myself in their shoes in such a way that I can fully embrace what is true for them. I learned that their first priority was to address what was most pressing at home or at work. If I could discover what these issues were, I could help them use new skills to successfully address these issues. That would enable them to grow rapidly and take enthusiastic ownership of the process of becoming whole-brained. Their successes were linked to my role model as their student as we were all learning to listen below the surface and remove internal barriers. When I describe myself as their student, that meant that I, too, kept an action plan and was transparent about where I was working to improve. Frequently, Clients would tell me at the end of our call that one of the things they appreciated the most was my transparency about my own struggles and imperfections. This seemed to give them permission to open up even more with their own concerns and struggles.

In order to be our Client's students we had to ask ourselves some tough questions.

| Deborah Welch

## EXPLORE THE QUESTION, "AM I COACHABLE?"

This may seem like an unnecessary question, yet when asked in a safe place and an open spirit, surprising and useful information may emerge. Our family may provide painful yet valuable feedback. Teenagers can be brutally honest. Yet how can we expect those around us to respond to our coaching if we are not modeling a welcoming spirit and taking action to correct errors once we have been provided respectful coaching? We add the descriptor *respectful* because rude, abrasive, or combative feedback triggers defensiveness. Both the giver and the receiver of feedback can benefit by being self-aware of how we participate in both roles—giving and receiving feedback and taking appropriate action in response.

| Duane Trammell

## FIVE COACHING QUESTIONS

As a way of priming the pump, so to speak, these coaching questions effectively open and invite a healthy dialogue. We have offered these queries to leaders as suggested questions to make it safe for those reporting to them to risk giving meaningful feedback and improve trust and healthy teaming.

1. What am I doing (or not doing) that contributes to your best performance?

2. What am I doing (or not doing) that undermines your best performance?

3. What am I doing that you would like to do or learn to do?

4. When and how do I tend to micromanage?

5. When and how do I "shoot the messenger"?

Most of us would never intentionally micromanage or shoot the messenger. But what we view as appropriate, careful coaching may be received as unnecessary and dismissive. In the same way, an attempt to provide additional information around a team outcome and involving the whole team in processing a team misstep may be experienced as shooting the messenger.

| Ann McGee-Cooper

## REFRAMING TOXIC LANGUAGE

I have learned in active listening to respectfully reframe what I call toxic language so the person can hear what it might sound like to bring respect to their concerns and feelings. For example, if a person said, "I hate these idiots I work with. They are driving me crazy!" I might rephrase this to be, "So you are highly frustrated with the lack of action and attention to detail by those you work with and it sucks your energy dry! As a result you feel really hostile. Am I hearing your right?" If I am missing the point, they will correct me. Once we hit the mark, they feel affirmed, and we can move forward. Toxic language typically is abusive to self and others. Learning to assume goodwill to self and others is step one in servant leadership. You can't give to others what you haven't given to yourself. And once you learn to honor your own feelings and transform them to become valid yet respectful of all parties, you have many positive opportunities for transformation.

| Ann McGee-Cooper

## GIVE OWNERSHIP FOR THE PROCESS

We learned that what didn't work was for someone to obediently put in their time with me but take no ownership. The most effective way to give a person ownership was to send him a draft agenda (suggesting that we begin by celebrating progress and breakthroughs, harvesting any lessons learned, and then processing new concerns) and then ask what he wanted to focus on. I started the hour with a brief check-in to see what was going on for him, then I asked how he wanted to focus the time. By addressing the Client's agenda and not mine, I am able to establish his ownership. After asking what would be the most valuable way to use this time, I have had a Client say, "I really need to leave and get X done now. I am in such a crisis." I offered to give him back the hour and either reschedule or not. Once Clients know that the choice is theirs, I rarely have had anyone not choose to reschedule and come back at a more convenient time. I have learned that forced coaching is not effective. It wastes the time of both parties. So don't be afraid of giving the choice to the person being coached.

To serve as a coach is a sacred process based on mutual trust. The foundation of success is the importance of the Client choosing me as their coach and ensuring that I've not imposed on them in any way. Often, when we work with a senior leader, we are brought in to take a team of senior leaders through one or two years of transformation as we teach the skills of servant leadership and high-performance teaming. As a part of that process, we offer coaching for each participant to adopt a personal action plan created by that individual in the class session. As we get started, I have found it very important to make sure people are welcoming this support. If not, I have learned it is far better to respectfully walk away from the coaching relationship, making sure they had other choices. I can sense if a person is obediently complying with the program as opposed to bringing a readiness to authentically transform. The journey of self-awareness requires great courage. That has to be chosen from within. This whole process must be entered into with the right spirit by both parties. It's not a failure to step back from the coaching relationship. Timing is everything, and demonstrating a sincere respect for the person's readiness without judgment is essential.

> **"To serve as a coach is a sacred process based on mutual trust."**

| Ann McGee-Cooper

## COACHING DOESN'T WORK EVERY TIME

Perhaps you, the reader, are imagining that every opportunity to coach ends with success. Let us share some of our "failures" and what we are learning from them.

Both of these examples involved personal shortcomings which significantly limited a gifted professional's performance. I was asked by the chairman/CEO in each situation to work with the professional in the hope of improving performance. One person was at the very top of his organization. The other was an individual contributor. They were offered coaching time with me to help them grow new skills in remedial areas.

In the case of the senior executive, I explained why I was there and asked permission to shadow this person to see what I could learn. After several site visits, I asked to share my observations. The COO was very bright, an intuitive leader, and intimidating in size and communication style. He used sarcasm as a weapon and could reduce the other person into a defensive position in an instant.

I explained to him that he was triggering a neural hijack (a huge flood of adrenaline in the brain due to fear, anger, or anxiety). As we learned in chapter 4, a person gets "very strong and very dumb" as 70 percent of the blood leaves the brain and shoots into the arms and legs so the person can run or fight. I explained to my friend that he was literally causing his direct reports to appear dumb when, in fact, they were very capable outside of his presence. His communication style could be classified as verbal abuse in that it humiliated, shamed, and insulted his managers with demeaning language. He was undermining their confidence, and it was a classic situation of self-fulfilling prophecy.

> "I can't inspire positive change unless the person being encouraged to change sees a benefit in doing so."

The senior executive looked at me with eyes flashing and said, "Ann, with what I pay each of these managers, I can treat them any way I choose to." And unfortunately, he was right. But he would also pay a price for his critical attack on his team's self-esteem. He would never know their true value or what they potentially could contribute. I learned that I can't inspire positive change unless the person being encouraged to change sees a benefit in doing so. My first and most important challenge is to qualify upfront by *listening for* a person's desire and willingness to make changes in areas that have been flagged for improvement. There must be authentic interest in changing from toxic behaviors and replacing them with more healthy, servant-led behaviors.

In the second example, the person had been an individual contributor (with little supervision) for approximately ten years. Recently, he had been assigned to report to a senior manager. It soon became clear that he lacked many key skills necessary to contribute in a high-performing organization. He was told the importance of these skills and that his continuing employment was contingent on his professional growth. We worked together in several sessions, yet there was little or no improvement. I learned that he was perhaps only giving lip service to the opportunity to work with a coach. Since his job depended on his agreeing to work with me, he chose to do so. Yet his heart was not in it. He either didn't believe he needed to change his behavior or he wasn't willing to make the effort. He was given examples of what project management and communication skills were missing and how it might look with these new skills in place. Missing skills were broken down into bite-sized chunks, and he was walked through how to use them. There were many initiatives to encourage and support his growth. Yet he never followed up on any of the coaching he was offered.

> **"Focusing my best effort to discern whether there is a good fit based on mutual trust and intent is critical for long-term success."**

Reflecting on this situation, I was guilty of wanting to believe this Employee was invested in the process when, in fact, he believed the problem was with others who didn't appreciate his value. I realize now that he had worked without supervision for almost a decade and resented having a supervisor "holding him accountable." Again, the pattern became clear. I cannot succeed in helping others grow unless they believe there is a need for them to grow and a personal benefit for making the effort.

Now I try to talk new Clients out of working with me. I have learned that unless they can persuade me that they have the will, courage, and commitment to face shortcomings, get curious about more effective habits and skills, and then have the discipline to practice and put new skills in place, I should not accept the assignment. By declining the assignment before we begin, I leave the door open for the person to choose to work with another coach in the future. If I make a bold effort, only to fail, the Client may believe, "I tried this once and it didn't work." Focusing my best effort to discern whether there is a good fit based on mutual intent and mutual trust is a critical foundation for potential long-term success.

| Ann McGee-Cooper

## PLUS/DELTA: INVITING TWO-WAY LEARNING

One of the most valuable practices for me has been to save the final three to five minutes for the Client to coach me. I use a PLUS/DELTA process. By *plus,* I mean what has been most valuable to you on this call and why. And *deltas* are the opportunities to grow and improve. How can I continue to grow as your coach? Are there ways I can improve the value of our time together? This practice helps me tailor my work to the individual, and also, it surfaces patterns of growth for me. For example, I am very right-brained and comfortable working spontaneously. Yet most of our Clients are dominant left-brained and prefer an agenda with no surprises; therefore, sending a suggested agenda in advance is appreciated by most Clients. However, many dominant right-brained people prefer to be in the moment and trust that

> **By modeling my eagerness to grow from their feedback, my input becomes a gift rather than an imposition."**

the most critical questions will automatically emerge. Often, the Client will invite me to talk about any deltas they might benefit from working on. By patiently modeling my eagerness to grow from their feedback and waiting for their invitation, my input becomes a gift to them rather than an imposition.

| Deborah Welch

## THE LADDER OF INFERENCE

At the core, it is vital to discover how to grow relationships and harmonize with others so that we aren't misdirecting our strengths but instead are discovering the best that is possible between us. One tool that I use year after year is the Ladder of Inference. [42]

Mental models are the images, assumptions, and stories that we carry in our minds. They shape the way we see things. Our old mental models become self-reinforcing and limit us from seeing others and ourselves as we truly are. Chris Argyris, a one-time Harvard professor, developed the Ladder of Inference tool as a way to understand differences in perceptions—the mental pathways that lead us to misguided beliefs. In any conversation or situation, we have an opportunity to go back down the Ladder of Inference, see more clearly, and arrive at common ground.

To explain how this works, imagine that we each have a ladder. In any one discussion, we go up that ladder, and other participants go up their own ladders. Often, it is as if we are leaning our ladders on different buildings, and by the time each of us gets up to the top of our own ladder, we can be far away from the specific details of what occurred in a discussion. Imagine trying to understand someone whose ladder has taken him or her to the top of a whole different building. We barely hear that person at all. Moving up the ladder works as described in the illustration on the next page.

**"Our old mental models become self-reinforcing and limit us from seeing others and ourselves as we truly are."**

## The Ladder of Inference

**4**

Finally, we reach the top of the ladder as we make a decision for action. By the time we are on top of the ladder we may be far away from the reality of what was actually said.

**3**

Then we climb up another rung on the ladder. We make assumptions about the data and the meaning. No two people hold the same identical assumptions about life, and, like fish in water, we may be the last ones to see our own assumptions and blind spots. However, based on those assumptions, we draw conclusions.

**2**

We move up the ladder with this data by adding meaning to it. It means something to us based on our prior personal and cultural experiences. We see this data through a filter.

**1**

We begin with an observation. We draw from a discussion specific data that has meaning for us. The words and ideas we select may be very different from the ones selected by another individual in the discussion.

In their book, *Dialogue: Rediscover the Transforming Power of Conversation,* Linda Ellinor and Glenna Gerard illustrate the Ladder of Inference with this story and show how perceptions can take different tracks in a real-life situation:[43]

- Sally walks into a meeting a little late and doesn't make eye contact with me.

- Sally is not saying why she is avoiding eye contact (select data).

- I've had others avoid eye contact, and it meant they didn't agree or they think I'm off base (add meaning).

- Sally thinks what I have to say isn't important (make assumptions).

- Sally doesn't care enough to even say what she is thinking (draw conclusions).

- I'm not going to work with Sally as much on any key tasks (decide on action).

By the end of the meeting, it may seem that Sally and I have not even been in the same meeting. There are hundreds of possible scenarios for why Sally may have arrived late and not made eye contact, but the individual selects things out based on the thought processes that occurred.

Anytime you feel inner or outer conflict, it's helpful to pause and explore your assumptions. You can take yourself through the steps of the Ladder of Inference by filling out a page like this (starting at the bottom):

5. Actions I decided on_____

4. Conclusions I drew _____

3. Assumptions I made _____

2. Meaning I added _____

1. Observations and data I selected _____

It always amazes me how often I benefit from coming back down the ladder. Almost any time I find myself having trouble understanding someone else's views clearly, there may be a blind spot that I have or an old story I am running through my mind that's blocking me from seeing new possibilities.

| Ann McGee-Cooper

## PRACTICES TO ENHANCE ENERGY (CELEBRATION AND APPRECIATION)

Our culture, especially our business culture, seems very uncomfortable with celebrations and mirroring each other's strengths. An authentic, creative celebration of individuals and teams generates the energy to keep pressing forward. When we only focus on where we need to improve, we can begin to slow down under the weight of "try hard" rather than enjoying the momentum of frequent celebrations mixed with "lessons learned" and continuous aggressive improvement.

One of the keys to providing constructive celebration and appreciation is to make it specific and authentic. "Good job" is rarely as effective as, "Your writing style is funny, insightful, and carefully validated by specific data. You consistently create very powerful messages that give credit to specific members of your team and bring strong credibility to our brand. Thank you!" By providing specific details based on what was done and why it is beneficial, the receiver is less likely to resist accepting it as honest. In other words, speak both to the left brain (specific, clear, measurable data) and to the right brain (emotions, appreciation, validation of effort, and attitude).

| Ann McGee-Cooper

## AN ENERGIZING HABIT AT THE END OF YOUR WORKDAY

In the spirit of celebration, on the way home from work only tell yourself what you did right or well that day. Learn to park frustration and failure to be harvested only when you are refreshed. Fatigue typically causes us to exaggerate the negative and to be unable to find the positive. So instead, make it your practice to celebrate any accomplishments on the way home from work. As you do this, you will be amazed at how much you do every day that goes unnoticed and unappreciated by you. The other benefit is a growing sense of entitlement to a refreshing and fun evening.

One day I arrived at work an hour early, worked through lunch, and stayed an hour late. On my commute home, I was so discouraged. On reflection, I had accomplished nothing on my lengthy to-do list while adding several new assignments. When I explored this with a coach, I discovered that my to-do list was made up primarily of paperwork, yet my work as a leader was primarily about coaching and supporting people. I was encouraged to practice this new habit of celebrating my accomplishments both large and small at the end of my work day.

At first it was really difficult. I found it hard to come up with even one thing to celebrate. I kept focusing on what went wrong or didn't get done. And then, little by little, I began to recognize the many small acts of kindness, perseverance, service, and creativity that filled my day. Little by little, I began to feel a sense of pride and ownership of each full, demanding, and resourceful day of generous service. I began to feel entitled to some time off, some "me time," some fun and renewal once I got home. I was a single mom, so there was dinner to prepare and many chores. But I decided to take time to shoot baskets and have some fun with my teenage son. Then he pitched in and helped with the chores. I was amazed at how my energy, attitude, and life changed.

| Ann McGee-Cooper

## THE CHALLENGES OF CELEBRATION

Years ago I had a very powerful senior leader I was coaching who worked in a tough and dangerous industry. At the end of one of our calls, he said to me, "Ann, you waste my time being nice. I prefer the unvarnished truth. Just spit it out, warts and all. I can take it, and besides, you confuse me and waste my time protecting me from the truth."

I summarized what I heard him saying to make sure I was clear about his request. "So you find it annoying and a waste of time when I use so many words. You are asking me to be more direct and candid. Please don't try to protect your feelings. You will handle that part, and you feel insulted when I dilute the truth with diplomacy. Am I hearing you right?" "You got it!" he assured me.

Well, as I prepared for the next call, I practiced a great deal on this because I have worked hard to be honest yet respectful. I realized that I would fail in his eyes if I didn't take his request seriously. I even asked a Client who was also very tough and direct to help me get all the cushioning niceties out of my dialogue. Our next call went really well, I thought. I was frank, direct, to the point, and I thought he was appreciative. When we got to the close and I asked for his PLUS/DELTA evaluation, I was stunned. His voice changed slightly as he got quiet and said something like this: "Well, you obviously listened when I asked you to drop all the mealy-mouth coddling and get right to the point. You took the wind out of me a couple of times." There was a long silence, and I was anxious and puzzled. He broke the silence by saying in a softer voice, "I think I could learn better if you don't mind going back to your former style. I found myself protecting my ego rather than listening for a new way to see situations. I guess I never realized why you did what you did."

> " In every call, I find a gift of wisdom, a mirror of possibility, an insight that helps me grow."

I had a good laugh at myself. All through the call, I thought I was earning his respect and was clearly working very hard to stay in character as direct, frank, and unprotective of his feelings. I truly thought I was speaking his language and that he would applaud that I had respected his request. I was totally caught off guard when he asked that I shift back into my former style. Yet I truly believe that if I hadn't done my best to honor his coaching of me, I might have lost his trust and respect. In every call, I find a gift of wisdom, a mirror of possibility, an insight that helps me grow. This is definitely a two-way street with a gifted, committed learning Partner joining me in the adventure of self-discovery. For me, this transforms this interaction. And I thank Robert Greenleaf for first modeling this and then inspiring me to listen to my intuition and to the intuitive wisdom in each person I engage in a dialogue of growth as a servant-leader.

| Ann McGee-Cooper

## DISCOVERY OF THE POWER WITHIN

I believe we are all potential coaches, and a significant discovery for me was to realize with utmost humility that everyone around me is a potential coach for me. If there is one thing I could change in my life, it would be to invite and welcome more coaching. When I was an art teacher in elementary school, I invited the children to coach me. Consistently, they provided valuable clues to help me grow in my role as teacher. Through their eyes, I realized that they had all the wisdom they needed, and that I could give them an even greater gift than advice, no matter how sage, by helping them to learn to hear and trust their own inner wisdom. Introducing the kids to their own inner voice was a profound step for them in their process of emotional maturity. The challenge for them was to discover how to get out of their own way.

When we begin to respect that each of us has something very powerful to contribute and that each of us needs the reflections and support of those around us, this is the discovery of the power of collaboration, community, and high-performance teaming. When you form a synergistic partnership with others with the intent to support the best outcome for self *and* the team, something magical emerges that no one can ever quite explain.

I am drawn to the quote from Humberto Maturana, an internationally respected Chilean biologist and philosopher, "The only emotion that expands intelligence is love."[44] So I have learned to dare to bring love into everything I do. What does it mean to love one's self unconditionally? For me, it means to have compassion for my imperfection without collapsing into self-defeating behaviors. It means daring to have bold dreams and then to live into them.

*Nothing much happens without a dream. And for something really great to happen, it takes a really great dream. Behind every great achievement is a dreamer of great dreams.*

—Robert Greenleaf

We all long to enjoy our bold dreams, both as delicious fantasies and then as exciting possibilities that we can courageously make real. So many people don't realize that their bold dreams are their genius calling to them. Getting to participate in this transforming discovery is what it means to be a servant-leader coach.

There is one other quote I'd like to share. In the opening interview with Bob Gary, Former Executive Vice President of Generation for Texas Utilities and a wise mentor, Client, and friend who was our first major corporate Client in 1985, I noticed this quote on his desk:

> *It's what you do now when you don't have to do anything that makes you what you want to be when it's too late to do anything about it.*

> —**Robert J. Gary**

It was something he lived by and encouraged all his team to join him in. It has become the cornerstone of our challenge—to not only teach self-actualization and servant leadership but to live it to the best of our ability.

## "The only emotion that expands intelligence is love."
—*Humberto Maturana*

# CONCLUSION

ALTHOUGH EVERY COACH has a unique style of coaching, the stories, ideas, and practices of servant leadership coaching exhibit some essential elements. In this chapter we share ideas for bringing this all together. We also invite you to reflect on how you measure progress in your own growth as a servant-leader coach. And finally, we offer some ideas for action. Here are some key takeaways as a start.

Servant leadership requires a journey of self-discovery. And stories are one of the most effective ways to learn not just about the outer landscape of leadership but about our inner landscape as well. We have shared some of the stories that have helped us and our Clients and Partners move from being reactive to proactive or from telling to listening. Just by exploring stories, we relax a little more and create a safe space for someone else to hear his or her own inner wisdom. When we allow more time for discovery, we find that looking back years later we couldn't have predicted the good that comes from time for reflection and inner learning. It is as Joseph Jaworski said:

> "If we are willing to take that most difficult journey toward self-discovery and lifelong learning, we will lead lives filled with meaning."

*Commitment is not, as I once thought, doing whatever it takes to make things happen. It is, rather, a willingness to listen, yield, and respond to the inner voice that guides us toward our destiny. . . . If we are willing to take that most difficult journey toward self-discovery and lifelong learning, we will lead lives filled with meaning. Moreover, we will gain the capacity to create and shape the future for ourselves and our organizations in ways we can hardly imagine.*[45]

Time for self-discovery doesn't have to mean weeks of silent reflection; it can happen every time we take a moment to stop and reflect. For example, in appendix B there is a story from Steve Parker who asks himself the simple question, "Am I too busy to lead?" He confronts an illusion that is so easy to fall into: the "I have a lot on my plate" mentality. A shift in perspective from time to time is how he grows. He chooses to remember to refocus on "being the servant-leader I want to be." He chooses to dialogue more and says, "The more time I spend conveying principles, goals, and what is important, the less I have to engage in the day-to-day issues (like putting out fires). And then the more time I have to invest in leading in a way that matters. As I relax, my team members relax and become far more effective."

A key message we hope you will take from this book is that we are much more connected with our team members, Partners, and Clients than we realize.

| Ann McGee-Cooper

## THE POWER OF COACHING RELATIONSHIPS

One thing that distinguishes coaching as a servant-leader is portrayed in the credo by Robert Greenleaf found in his book *The Institution as Leader*: "This is my thesis: caring for persons, the more able and the less able serving each other, is the rock upon which a good society is built."[46]

It has been our experience that one never helps another grow without receiving a mutual gift from this experience. Hearing the innermost wisdom of another and witnessing the courage to transform awakens our own desire to look inward and dare to grow also. Bringing true humility into this process and realizing that the greatest gifts emerge not from the coach but from the coaching relationship and the courage to ask questions takes each of us deeper. We believe this is the spirit to which Robert Greenleaf was pointing.

With servant leadership coaching, greatness grows over time, sometimes more than we even realize. Here is a story by Cliff and Maddie Watson illustrating the power of the coaching relationship. (At this time, Cliff was Director of Generation, Southern Region, Luminant and his daughter, Maddie, was a junior at Dallas Baptist University.)

## CROSSING THE FINISH LINE: THE VISION OF SUCCESS | Cliff Watson

MY TWENTY-YEAR-OLD DAUGHTER, Madison ("Maddie"), decided in October that she wanted to run a half marathon (13.1 miles). I had run long distance races before and was thrilled that she wanted to move from "spectator" to "participant." She decided to run The Cowtown Half Marathon scheduled for the following February. She located a training schedule and started the process. Madison is a college student and lives away from home. Although she was faithful to start the training process on her own, we started running together while she was home for

Christmas break. We enjoyed training as a pair and decided to run the half marathon together.

Our weekly running schedule included progressively longer runs on Saturdays. The furthest distance Maddie had previously run was 10K (6.2 miles), so anything longer than that was a new experience. The difficulty of running longer distances was compounded following a seasonal illness that affected her breathing. A couple of miles into the six-mile run, she started slowing down and then started walking. When I checked on her, I saw that she was crying. She told me to go on and that she would find her way home. I told her we were in this thing together, and I would go at whatever pace she could stand. As we continued the run-walk-cry pace that day, I asked her to envision the two of us crossing the finish line at the Cowtown Half Marathon ... holding hands ... arms raised high. I wasn't sure she was listening as I received little response.

> **I just keep thinking about us crossing the finish line ... holding hands ... arms raised high.**

Maddie recovered from the illness but encountered other obstacles along the way, including bitter cold training days and a knee injury. We incorporated stops in each long run to allow her to rest and stretch. With each obstacle, I tried to encourage her again to envision the two of us crossing the finish line at The Cowtown Half Marathon ... holding hands ... arms raised high. I didn't receive the response I was hoping for, but at least she was still running.

At last, race day came. As was typical for our long training runs, we agreed to stop at mile six to stretch and take a water break plus more frequently if she needed to. Our measure of success was to finish the race together but not worry about how long it would take.

As we approached the midway point, Maddie told me she didn't want to stop. I was quite surprised and asked her why not. Her response absolutely made my day. She responded, "I just keep thinking about us crossing the finish line ... holding hands ... arms raised high!"

We finished the race that day. It was a milestone day for me personally in that I was able to experience, first-hand, my daughter's fulfillment of a goal. The picture was much broader, however. I realized that she had, after all, grasped the imaging challenge I had tried to encourage her with. From a father's perspective, it was a tremendous encouragement to know that she had listened to and embraced this important life lesson of holding a vivid picture of desire in her mind and then finding a way to create it successfully—a practice she will be able to use in any area of life that she encounters.

## THE END IS THE REWARD | Maddie Watson

TRAINING FOR THIS HALF MARATHON tested me to the core. There were countless times that I wanted to quit training or whine about my knee or illness or weather (which I'm sure I did whine about at times). But my dad was there every step of the way encouraging me and holding me accountable. There is a quote that my dad often uses: "Begin with the end in mind." Countless times, my dad would unknowingly encourage me with that simple statement. The journey is not always a fun, easy-going ride; it is not always enjoyable. In my case, training through freezing weather, bronchitis, allergies, blisters, and a knee injury was not fun, but crossing the finish line on race day, hand-in-hand with my dad, made everything so worth it. I would envision crossing the finish line with him when I didn't want to run anymore and when I wanted to quit training, and that vision kept me going. Sometimes, when I really wanted to quit, I would envision what race day would be like with me on the sidelines as a spectator. I knew that I would be so disappointed in myself for leaving my dad to train and run by himself. I did not want to do that to him. I learned to always begin whatever journey I embark on with the end in mind. The end is the vision. The end is the reward.

It's not every day that you hear about a fifty-one-year-old man running a half marathon with his twenty-year-old daughter. As a result of my dad's work to learn servant leadership at the executive level, I have seen him grow more confident and effective in his leadership skills. And he has been able to pour his new skills back out to his family and friends.

Looking back I now realize that I had begun to fall into the mindset that I am just a college student, so nothing I do matters. But now I realize that this is not the case. Rather than waiting until I "grow up," I realize that I have many opportunities to make a positive difference in the lives of others right now. I am spreading my wings.

| Deborah Welch

## CALL FORTH GREATNESS

Cliff and Maddie's story illustrates powerfully how, through relationships, we can coach each other to step into our best selves and call forth greatness in each other. Meg Wheatley puts it this way: "People make a commitment to be there for each other; they participate not only for their own needs, but to serve the needs of others. . . . [Then] the speed at which people learn and grow is noteworthy."[47]

If you leave this book with only one main takeaway, we hope we have made a strong case that if you are serious about being a servant-leader you can't do it without learning Partners. And in any learning partnership, a key will be to develop servant-leader coaching capacities. We have summarized these ideas in the chart in appendix A and offer it as a tool that could be useful for creating a shift in mind or choosing actions to take based on the principles in this book.

After you review the chart, we invite you to make your own chart—your own "best test" of servant leadership coaching. We have found that servant-leader coaches can benefit by taking this list and building on it, considering their own aspirations and purpose in coaching, making their own list of guiding ideas, and reviewing it prior to a coaching opportunity. We encourage you to experiment with this chart.

Another approach that has worked well is to think about individuals in your life who are or could be learning Partners. This can be a family member, a friend, a mentor, or a professional coach. Seeking out individuals who have different strengths from our own, exploring servant leadership coaching with a Partner, or finding someone new to connect with can be powerful. We have reflected on what helps accelerate the process of servant-leader growth. It is counterintuitive that it is the small, marginal changes that make the biggest difference. We never do it perfectly. But by taking time for discovery, progress toward the greatest leadership goals happen more quickly.

The essential ideas put forth in this book are about a way of being that we choose as coaches. We are on a journey of growth. We don't just gain information and implement it like we do when learning computer skills. This work of servant leadership coaching requires an enormous commitment and an openness of the heart. Progress doesn't always happen in the logical steps we plan. More often it occurs through unexpected twists and turns, and we come to it kind of sideways. We may feel we are going backward, only later to learn that this is when we took the most important step forward. How do we stay focused and find markers that keep us on our path of development as a servant-leader coach? How do you measure progress?

Parker Palmer sheds some light on this:

> *I have learned to test myself not by "effectiveness" but to measure myself instead by "faithfulness." I ask myself, "Have I been as faithful as I know how to be to my gifts, to the needs of others, and to my best self?" The word "effectiveness" makes me small. I look to see if I have been true to my gifts and to what is possible between myself and others. I don't look to control but to foster and cultivate something great.* [48]

In many ways being "faithful" and "cultivating something great" is about caring enough to discover what is possible between our Partners and ourselves. This takes unusual focus and capacity building not often discussed in leadership books. Otto Scharmer calls this lack of inner awareness "the blind spot of leadership" because we know a lot about what leaders do but little about what happens inside them, their interior condition, their experiences with self-awareness, and how they discover their best selves. Through deeper levels of seeing and attention, great social possibilities arise. Leadership is not about control. It is about responsibility and accountability that is based in caring feedback and a deeper source of connection. In the most life-giving moments, as in the case of Maddie and Cliff's story, it feels like awakening to a situation where unexpectedly things get easier. Sometimes a door that was closed to our Partner opens and things become easier.

> "Through deeper levels of seeing and attention, great social possibilities arise."

This journey of growing as a servant-leader coach feels like being "sharply awake and reasonably disturbed," as Greenleaf put it. Greenleaf pointed out that caring once happened mainly person to person, but now we must consider how it is mediated through institutions.

> *Institutions are often large, complex, powerful, impersonal; not always competent; sometimes corrupt. If a better society is to be built, one that is more just and more loving, one that provides greater creative opportunity for its people, then the most open course is to raise both the capacity to serve and the very performance as servant . . . by new regenerative forces.*[49]

Regenerative forces of passion, purpose, and caring are at the core of servant leadership coaching. As we embrace these principles and work with others to create a two-way, ongoing learning process, the benefits are transformative and ripple into all parts of our lives.

# APPENDICES

# ESSENTIAL PRACTICES FOR SERVANT LEADERSHIP COACHING

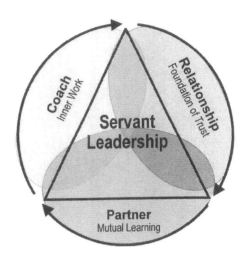

| Coaching with a Servant's Heart | | |
|---|---|---|
| | Is not | Is |
| **COACH:** Inner work | Coming to the coaching work with a cluttered or racing mind | Coming to the coaching work fully present and growing in self-awareness |
| | Asking others to take risks and grow while we sit on the sidelines; misunderstanding true humility | Knowing that humility is getting the ego out of the way to let our greatness be unleashed, which helps others do the same |
| | Ignoring our own strengths and gifts | Learning how to best use our strengths and gifts when we coach |
| | Forgoing or neglecting our own growth and having a fixed mindset where we judge others or ourselves | Remembering that our ability to be effective grows in proportion to our own growth; asking non-judgmental questions for self-discovery to grow as a coach |
| | Believing we have to have all the answers | Knowing we never have all the answers, but something happens in coaching that is often beyond our expectations |

| Coaching with a Servant's Heart | | |
|---|---|---|
| **PARTNER:**<br>Outer work in mutual learning | **Is not** | **Is** |
| | A hierarchical relationship in which the coach tells the other person how to achieve goals | Establishing that the relationship is non-hierarchical and mutual |
| | Owning the problem and process and trying to get the coachee to "buy in" on the solution | Person being coached owns the process |
| | Quick advice giving (Giving advice when it is not needed or in a way that precludes the person finding his or her own answers) | Listening deeply and asking good questions; helping the coachee feel supported to set self-accountabilities and surface blind spots and discover inner wisdom |
| | One size fits all style of teaching skills and processes | Attending to unique learning styles, unique gifts and strengths, and what energizes the person we are coaching |
| | Learned dependency on the coach as an expert | Asking for feedback: "How can I be most helpful to you?" (Plus/Delta) |

| Coaching with a Servant's Heart | | |
|---|---|---|
| **RELATIONSHIP:**<br>Foundation of Trust | **Is not** | **Is** |
| | Withholding our humanness; failing to discern how to best use stories as a coach | Sharing stories that expand insight and empathy; helping our coaching partner see we are all human |
| | Taking up all the "air time" in the conversation and filling any empty space in the conversation with words | Welcoming companionable silence; inviting insights that come from times of silence |
| | Keeping others at arm's length to deal with relational difficulties or alternatively sympathizing with others in a way that stifles their potential | Being genuinely empathic and building relational bonds |
| | Focusing on "fixing" the person | Recognizing the dignity and spirit of the person being coached; encouraging forgiveness so a new story can emerge, restoring trust and supporting progress toward growth |

We find this chart useful to assess how we are doing in our servant leadership coaching. We encourage you make this chart your own; change the words, add your own ideas, and even consider creating your own chart.

# APPENDIX B

## AM I TOO BUSY TO LEAD?

### By Steve Parker

Steve Parker is Director of Sandow Generation, a lignite plant in south central Texas, a part of Luminant Fossil Generation. Sandow has an operating capacity of 1,137 Megawatts, enough to power about 570,000 homes in normal conditions. Steve has been on a journey of leadership development, and in this recent letter to Ann, he shares the benefits of finding time for intentional leadership with his people at the plant.

---

### Steve's Letter to Ann

*During a coaching session with Ann McGee-Cooper, I mentioned that I was pondering the question, "Am I too busy to lead?" This question struck me as I realized the message I am unintentionally sending in my day-to-day rush to keep up with unit status, reading and responding to emails, and preparing for and attending meetings. People must quietly think, "Steve is too busy to hear or consider what I have to say." What a loss of opportunity when words and thoughts are never shared.*

*No question, I have a lot on my plate, but when I really think about it, I realize I am too focused on short-term reactionary management of the facility and not taking care of what is most important—what pays big dividends for everyone—"being the servant-leader I want to be."*

*I must do my day-to-day management job, but more importantly, I must focus the majority of my time on leading.*

*Leading is a whole lot more enjoyable and rewarding than managing, and I actually get more done through others when I choose to lead rather than do.*

*It is a fulfilling day when I take time to roam the halls, have lunch with employees, get to know individuals as people in a relaxed mode, and get an opportunity to understand their concerns. I focus on thinking a week ahead, who I want to spend time with the following week, who I want to get to know and grow. I am doing a better job of controlling my calendar and allotting time to lead. I am trying to do a better job of spending time with my wife and taking better care of myself. I have found that leading brings me energy, allowing me to be more effective and accomplish more.*

*I offer the following to help explain the trials and rewards I see day-to-day as I focus on being a leader first, serving those around me by showing interest in them as human beings, getting to know them, and understanding their ideas and barriers. I have learned my bandwidth multiplies when I take the opportunity to truly listen, communicate, understand, and work with the team to build a common purpose.*

*I get more done through others by leading, engaging, coaching, and growing those around me. It feels good to see team success and see individuals swell with pride when they succeed. I have to be mindful to ask questions and encourage dialogue rather than direct how, when, and where—my fallback when I am in a hurry. I find sharing stories about personal successes and failures helps me to share potential land mines to those I am talking with. I am building trust and confidence every time I take the time to slow down enough to invest in people.*

*I am learning just how important it is to smile and take the time needed, in a relaxed frame of mind, to delegate, to clearly define the goal, define the ditches, the feedback I expect, and time frame for feedback. I have learned the hard way the importance of taking time for dialogue to ensure effective communication.*

*When I am relaxed, my team is relaxed. Just as HPI (Human Performance Improvement) tools slow us down to do the right things the right way, leading rather than managing allows us to get it right the first time, and then we don't have to go back and clean up mistakes. The more time I spend conveying principles, goals, and what is important, the less I have to engage in the day-to-day issues, allowing me more time to look forward.*

*I have an agreement with my team that they can call me out just as I call them out. It is working beautifully as we have trust and respect as our common bond. We care about each other first, we take care of each other, and we know we can count on each other.*

*I have always worked very hard to treat people as I would want to be treated, and I have been involved in listening to leadership audiobooks. What I haven't done is slow down enough to relax, take time to smile, and enjoy the people I work with. Servant leadership is helping me to be a better leader and that is very rewarding.*

*Thanks to Luminant for providing servant leadership training.*

*Servant leadership is inspiring me to be the leader I have always wanted to be.*

*Thanks,*

*Steve*

**" . . . we have trust and respect as our common bond. We care about each other first, we take care of each other, and we know we can count on each other."**

# APPENDIX C

## SAMPLE COACHING NOTES

Sometime over the years, it occurred to me to send a summary of our coaching conversations in the form of an email. Because of my dyslexia, I learned early to take notes while listening so I can stay focused. Also, it enhances my memory and insight. If I can go back and review careful notes, often I experience a leap of insight. So I respectfully ask my Partner's permission to send a summary along with the request that the receiver edit and confirm, change, or add to my notes. I also ask what format would be most helpful. Narrative seems to be the choice of the vast majority, yet a few prefer brevity in the form of bullets.

*A typical follow-up letter might include*

- ☐ **A summary of personal notes** (perhaps the person is planning an important vacation or just experienced an important family event). This sometimes becomes a backdrop for other insights.

- ☐ **Celebrations of progress** when practicing new skills learned in our team sessions and developing skills of servant leadership. These often happen with family members as well as on the job.

- ☐ **Reporting** from their personal action plan. What they chose. What they tried. What brought positive results. What may have brought up questions, concerns, or more complex challenges.

- ☐ **Current challenges** either at home or at work.

I reflect back as much of their narrative as I was able to catch. Many times I reframe toxic language into healthy language. For example, if someone said, "I have a terrible memory and feel like an idiot when I can't recall someone's name," I might reframe this as, "So honoring the people around you is an important personal value, and you disappoint yourself when you are unable to immediately recall someone's name. Am I hearing you right?" They seem to not only appreciate the respect I bring to their story but are able to shift into a more respectful frame of mind as they continue. I am modeling "assuming goodwill" and learning to "be gentle with yourself," two of the practices that lead to a more healthy and productive emotional maturity. It's difficult to be open to learning when you feel blamed and labeled as wrong or bad; that promotes defensiveness.

> **By planting seeds of hope and possibility, we all seem to grow with greater confidence."**

Should I want to make side observations, I change the color of the font to be clear who is speaking. Often I am lifting up a pattern of inner wisdom that I see reflected in the notes after the call. In essence, I am mirroring: "You seem to have a strong sense of what you don't want to continue doing and also a strong commitment to grow. You might stay curious to what is getting in your way. You celebrated several significant positive outcomes from practicing active listening. Perhaps you are growing faster than you realize. Stay curious." By planting seeds of hope and possibility, we all seem to grow with greater confidence.

At the end of every call I save three to five minutes for a PLUS/DELTA. This is a time for us to reflect together on the quality of this time together. PLUS: What brought the greatest value to this call for you? And DELTA: How can I continue to grow as your coach and enhance the value of this time in the future? I have learned to welcome my Partners' coaching, especially corrective coaching. No matter what it is, my job is to model welcoming this opportunity to learn through their eyes. It isn't always easy, but every instance of coaching has taught me so much. And the pattern of feedback over the years has shaped my practice and skills.

## Inviting Clients to Send a Summary

Two years ago when I was diagnosed with breast cancer, I knew that I must find ways to work fewer hours. Even though I loved my work, I needed more time to rest, so I began to reevaluate each part of my day. One of the early changes I made was to invite Clients I was coaching to create their own summary of our meetings and share it with me. Previously, I had written a summary of each coaching call and shared it with the Client.

To my amazement and delight, I have discovered that what each Client writes and shares is much more valuable than having me draft it for them. First, I learn what *they* heard and found valuable. And second, in the process of writing their notes, they are taking the learning deeper and making a personal commitment to grow and change. I am then able to comment and add any additional resources or insights. In every case, they have noted how helpful this practice has become since we both can "sleep on our dialogue" and then take it further as needed.

On the following pages is an example from one of the summaries.

**❝...those who follow through and make time to create and share their progress in any form seem to make significantly more progress in their growth as servant-leaders."**

Dear Ann,

I worked on my notes from the call three days later than I planned! Immediately I started feeling negative towards myself—why didn't I do it right away? I told Ann I'd do it after the call . . . I am late again . . . I carried notes with me to home and office back and forth, but I couldn't find time (oh, wait, that's an excuse. Stop that!) . . . When are you going to get stuff done when you promised? No one will rely on you . . .

And then I started transferring my notes from paper and laughed at myself. I realized that I am doing exactly what I need to work on—take responsibility, remember it for the future, do the work, but don't beat myself up.

1. So now I have positive energy—self-awareness and humor helped! Here are the notes: Talked about book "Healthy Selfishness" by Hellers.

2. Ann suggested using "self-valuing" versus "selfishness," correctly picking up that I have issues with negative aspects of selfishness. Value and appreciate myself first. Have the same respect for myself and same kindness towards myself like I would give others.

   When talking about being responsible and accountable and finding balance between responsibility and self-valuing, do not say, "It's my fault, I did it again, I am the bad one, how could I have?" Instead say, "I am taking responsibility, I made a mistake, but I want to get better and improve. So next time, I will do X." Focus on the future and correcting action rather than beating myself up and feeling shame and blame. Blaming myself is becoming a victim; taking responsibility is being accountable.

   When talking about making excuses versus giving reasons, excuses are when I explain myself but feel like I do not have to change. For example, believing that it is okay to keep doing what I have been doing.

   Stop being a judge and a critic. Become my own coach. A coach's goal is to improve the person, not beat her down.

A coach sees what you are doing right and points out respectfully things that you could be doing better.

3. With my children, become a positive role model. Play the game, "What do you feel proud of doing today? This week?" Start first and share what I am proud of. Be positive and value my efforts. Next invite them to do the same.

4. Stop using words such as "you always . . . ", "you never . . .", "you should. . . ." These are coercive, judgmental, and absolute. Instead use "I will", "I want to", "I can", "I get to." These are more positive and give me a choice.

5. Work-related, I shared my desire to do more to change things. Albert Einstein said, "You cannot continue to do the same thing and expect different results." Ann encouraged me to keep stretching and challenging myself to "get out of the box." I am excited to be moving in this direction!

I am very fortunate to have what I have, know people I know, live life the way I do. Thank you for being a part of my life.

I can tell you that each time I receive a summary, I am deeply moved. I never listen and ask clarifying questions but that I grow. I can often see myself in my Partners' challenges, and I typically find ways I want to grow as they commit to their Action Plan. This inner work continues to be a deeply healing blessing.

I have also included a more structured approach to this practice, the Kidwell Action Plan. Bob Kidwell, one of our engineering Clients, created a draft of his Action Plan and then added his notes in red to indicate his follow-through to-date. I was able to add my notes in a third color, and we had a clear record of our work. This process is most effective when the Action Plan is structured in a way that works best for each person. Some simply scan their written notes from our coaching call. Others create very brief bullets, and yet others use a narrative. I encourage a rough draft approach because the purpose is to remind us of progress, not be a formal report. It is kept confidential, only to be seen by the Client and me.

## KIDWELL ACTION PLAN

1. I will actively listen for and challenge blocking assumptions. Until these are visible and truly disproved, I will continue to struggle with inspiring a new group vision. *(Bob, I flagged the word choice, "struggle." By using the word struggle you set yourself up to struggle. What if you describe this to yourself as, "I will continue to stay engaged with inspiring the new group vision"? Can you hear a difference? AM-C)*

   - "We tried that once and it didn't work out" but not considering the context of the failed attempt.

   - "Management will never go for that" because of failed prior attempts where groundwork wasn't done and the idea wasn't "sold" properly.

   - "I have too much on my plate to put the quality in it," but we end up doing tasks two or more times because the quality was lacking on the initial attempt.

   - "They're too busy."

2. When we make excuses for those we serve, we send a negative message that our program is not important. If it isn't important to us, why should it be to anyone outside our group?

3. The ERO (emergency response organization) wants to be prepared, but sometimes they need us as an excuse to allow them to do what they know needs to be done (training/practice).

4. We need to become advocates for our program. If we don't believe in what we do or ask, we can never expect anyone outside our group to either. Project a realistic sense of importance and display confidence and our program will be better supported.

5. When discussing these topics with the group or individuals, make sure to use active listening to get the full picture on

the table first. If I challenge too soon, it can shut down communications or it may turn counterproductive as information comes out in bits and pieces. Get the whole picture defined and only then deal with it.

6. Perspective changes with position. While my focus has changed due to my increased responsibility, their focus might still be individual-based and not as much on the group. The work on defining a common vision needs to include elements to reveal these differences and align.

   - I admit the bad habits I've nourished in the group and will work with my staff to build ownership and accountability.
   - If I do it, who reviews it?
   - It shouldn't hit my desk until it's been reviewed by a peer. I'll answer any questions you have to ensure you start on the right path, but I won't be a co-developer.
   - More than three yellow stickies and it goes back to the author.
   - Team doesn't have to include me. I'm just the coach. Leadership should start with the "team captains" within the group.
   - Resist the urge to insist on perfect the first time. A good editor leaves a product that reflects the author, not the editor.

7. Continue building the team captains within the group.

8. Deal with resistance head on; do it positively and unemotionally, but don't shy away from it.

9. Speak to their greatness. Directly, indirectly, or round about, look at the message I convey about what I think they can accomplish. Let people rise to lofty expectations; don't weigh them down with negative feelings of mediocrity. The key is getting this energized within them and not imposing it from the outside

You can see two very different styles reflected in these two examples. Each has its benefits. What I appreciate the most is the ownership reflected in both pieces. We find that those who do follow through and make time to create and share their progress in any form seem to make significantly more progress in their growth as servant-leaders.

# APPENDIX D

# AUTHORS & CONTRIBUTORS

## AUTHORS

**Ann McGee-Cooper, Ed.D.,** is a business futurist, owns her own consulting company, and has worked with organizations for four decades in innovation, the politics of change, and servant leadership. She holds degrees from the University of Texas, Southern Methodist University, and a doctorate from Columbia University. Ann has worked in an unusually wide variety of workplaces—including coal mines of West Virginia, corporate boardrooms of international engineering and construction companies, the Culture Committee of Southwest Airlines, a NASCAR race team, and governmental agencies.

For her international work in servant leadership, Ann has been honored with two honorary doctorates from Trinity Western University and Sterling College. She also received the Good Neighbor Award from Southwest Airlines and was recognized by the International Professional Women's Alliance for pace-setting work in mentoring and servant leadership.

Ann has co-authored four books: *Building Brain Power, Being the Change: Profiles from Our Servant Leadership Learning Community, Time Management for Unmanageable People,* and *You Don't Have to Go Home from Work Exhausted!,* which has sold over one hundred thousand copies and been translated into four different languages. She also has written an Innovations in Management Series monograph, "The Essentials of Servant Leadership: Principles in Practice."

Ann believes in the power of servant leadership to transform business and all organizations, teams, and individuals. Since her first work with TDIndustries, Jack Lowe Sr., and Robert Greenleaf, she has dedicated her life to spreading the message of servant leadership. Ann lives each day by the inspiration of one of her earliest mentors, Dr. Margaret Mead: "Never doubt that a small group of thoughtful, committed citizens can change the world. Indeed, it is the only thing that ever has."

**Deborah Welch, Ph.D.,** coaches entrepreneurs and leaders in foundations, school districts, colleges, and corporations. Her studies of collaborative intelligence and of the very best of what is possible in leadership in organizations led her in 2008 to co-create, along with Ann McGee-Cooper and Virginia Gilmore, the first Virtual Servant Leadership Learning Community (VSLLC®). VSLLC® is a six-month program in which dedicated servant-leaders from around the world and across a variety of industries enhance their capacity to grow as servant-leaders and create connections for greater support in the work of servant leadership. In addition to serving in corporate and community e-learning and leadership coaching at AMCA, Deborah is also an award-winning faculty member at Capella University. She teaches The Psychology of Leadership and guides dissertation research in the area of self-awareness and leadership.

Deborah has published several articles. Most recently she co-wrote, "Strengths Based Leadership Coaching" with a research team, which has been published in Consulting Psychology Journal. Since there are no perfect servant-leaders, Deborah captured stories of the power of forgiveness in the workplace and published the book *Forgiveness at Work*. She brings a wide array of tools and processes into her coaching work based on several decades of experience. She is known for coaching that helps leaders achieve results and grow into their best selves. Deborah is humbled to work with dedicated leaders who are making a positive difference in the world.

**Duane Trammell, M.Ed.,** is founding Partner, President and COO of Ann McGee-Cooper and Associates, Inc. and has been collaborating with Ann for thirty-three years.

Duane enjoys writing, researching, and developing materials in servant leadership. He has co-authored *Time Management for Unmanageable People, You Don't Have To Go Home from Work Exhausted!, Being the Change: Profiles from Our Servant Leadership Learning Community*, and a second edition of *Awakening Your Sleeping Genius: A Journaling Approach to Personal Growth and Servant Leadership*. Trammell participated in Ann McGee-Cooper's early research on genius/giftedness and combined it with Robert Greenleaf's concepts on servant leadership to produce the journal.

Duane's expertise in leadership also expands into the community. For five years, he directed a leadership institute, which placed over 150 volunteers into the Dallas community in collaborations such as health fairs, community cleanups, and food and clothing drives for the needy.

As a business educator and leadership development specialist, Duane's specialty is writing and delivering participant-based learning. Educational awards have included "Dallas Teacher of the Year" and being named as "One of Three Outstanding Teachers in Texas."

## CONTRIBUTORS

**Dawna Markova, Ph.D.,** is internationally known for her groundbreaking work in helping people learn with passion and live on purpose. She is the co-founder and CEO Emeritus of Professional Thinking Partners, Inc. (PTP). She is an internationally known expert in the fields of asset-focused learning, cognitive psychology, and perception. Dawna is also a former Senior Affiliate of the Organizational Learning Center at MIT and a consultant member of the Society for Organizational Learning. She has established learning communities across the United States, leads workshops on maximizing individual and team talent, and serves as a thinking Partner to CEOs and senior executives around the world. She is the author of many books, including *Collaborative Intelligence: Thinking with People Who Think Differently, A Spot of Grace, I Will Not Die an Unlived Life, The Smart Parenting Revolution, The Open Mind* book and audio series, *No Enemies Within, How Your Child Is Smart,* and *Learning Unlimited.* She also co-edited *Random Acts of Kindness* and has been a frequent guest on National Public Radio. She is renowned for public speaking and has been hired by global organizations to deliver keynotes to thousands of participants.

**Cynthia Watson** has spent twenty-seven years in public service working for the federal government. During this time, she has worked more than twenty years in management. For the past ten years, Cynthia has worked as Regional Administrator, Southwest Region, Wage and Hour Division, Department of Labor. She is a member of the Senior Executive Service (SES), comprised of the men and women charged with leading the continuing transformation of government. Members of the SES serve in the key positions just below the top presidential appointees. SES members are the major link between these appointees and the rest of the federal workforce. Throughout her career, Ms. Watson has received numerous agency exceptional achievement awards, such as the Distinguished Career Service Award and the Dallas-Fort Worth Federal Executive Board's Nancy H. Doherty Federal Employee of the Year Award. She has a master's degree in organizational management and is a 2003 graduate of Harvard University's John F. Kennedy School of Government program for senior executive fellows. Cynthia has participated in the Virtual Servant Leadership Learning Community (VSLLC®) and, as a result of her participation, she has enriched and expanded her ideas about service. She has grown to appreciate the value of sharing vulnerability and sharing the journey and has been positively impacted in her professional and personal relationships.

**Rebecca Braden** is CEO of Cornerstone International, a firm that specializes in developing and coaching leaders and their teams in a wide variety of organizations worldwide. Rebecca has been an organizational consultant and executive coach for more than twenty years for both public and private sector professionals in their unique work environments. Her work has taken her to every continent except Antarctica. Rebecca's passion is servant leadership. She enjoys assisting leaders with recognizing, valuing, and drawing upon differences; creating feedback-rich environments; navigating through change and transition; and engaging in courageous conversations. Rebecca has been privileged to be a speaker and ambassador for the Greenleaf Center for Servant Leadership. She is the author of *Sanjaygawa and the Yak Whisperer*, gold-medal winner for Moonbeam Children's Book Awards. Her undergraduate education was pre-law at the University of Texas and her M.A. is in Organizational Psychology.

**Matthew Kosec** enthusiastically serves as an Adjunct Partner with Ann McGee-Cooper and Associates, Inc. Throughout his nearly sixteen-year career in law enforcement, he has sought growth opportunities and has found public service an excellent arena in which to grow leadership skills. Matt has been part of several creative policing teams, including the internationally recognized Carrollton Police Department Community Problem-Oriented Policing Team. Matt's varied responsibilities have helped him develop a wide variety of competencies, ranging from project management, to process improvement, to complete remodeling of learning systems. Matt serves on the Culture Committee of Southwest Airlines, where he has gathered insights into a leader-full organization as well as demonstrated his judging skills for chili cook-offs and talent for conga lines. Whether he is teacher, student, or somewhere in between, Matt can be relied upon to deliver insightfulness, academic credibility, and, most importantly, humor, in any learning environment. Matt has a master's degree in organizational leadership with a master's certificate in servant leadership. He is a graduate of the Police Executive Research Forum's Senior Management Institute for Police. He is also a graduate of the Virtual Servant Leadership Learning Community (VSLLC®) and has designed and co-facilitated curriculum for the VSLLC® program.

**Jenny Inge**—As a very young entrepreneur, Jenny followed a calling to the western mountains; landed in Creede, Colorado; and established Rare Things Gallery, a small business in a small town. Against all odds and thirty-five years later, the Gallery has become a major destination business and a cornerstone for Creede. What was once a small storefront and studio combination is now one of the finest and better known retail galleries in the Southwestern United States—a treasure trove of jewelry, antiques, decorative arts, photography, paintings, stained glass, pottery, woodwork, furniture, rocks, minerals, and wonderments of nature. Imagine living a life of passionate collecting, designing, and building in the magical mountains of Mineral County. Jenny believes "though Creede seems an impossible place to grow a business, I feel a direct line to the Creative Source here. I could not lead a richer life."

Best known for the Inge Horsehair Jewelry Collection, Jenny is also a skilled metal worker, multimedia artist, and savvy business proprietor. The mystique and lure of Rare Things makes the trek to Creede worthwhile. As Customers observe almost daily, Jenny has an amazing eye. You will often "see it first" at Rare Things, sometimes years before it hits the general market. Intriguing displays of unusual jewelry and collectibles invite lingering for hours. Energetic and knowledgeable personal shopping assistants bring life to the stories behind this global collection. A visit to the Gallery is always an adventure in treasure hunting.

**Shaunna Black** is Managing Partner of Venture Pacific Group International, LLC, a global advisory firm specializing in cross-border initiatives. Venture Pacific Group (VPG) accelerates business success for its Clients by sourcing global opportunities and growing business-to-business partnerships through its global network. VPG builds sustainable relationships with their Clients, understands their business strategy, designs solutions to accelerate their business growth, and nurtures new global partnerships. Shaunna leads the team in global operations. For the past eighteen years she has worked internationally in twenty-five countries. Formerly, Shaunna was President of Shaunna Black and Associates, a global operations firm. In her tenure with Texas Instruments, Inc. (TI), she also served as Vice President and Manager of Worldwide Environmental, Safety and Health, Manager of Dallas Semiconductor Manufacturing (DFAB), and Manager of Worldwide Facilities. Her experience in these roles gave her in-depth knowledge of manufacturing operations, facilities design, construction, and operation of TI facilities worldwide. In addition, she was responsible for environmental, safety, and health programs; worldwide security programs; real estate management; and TI's sustainability strategy. Ms. Black is currently a member of the Executive Advisory Board for the UT-Austin Engineering College. She is also a member of the board of directors for YWIRE Technologies, a Canadian company specializing in broadband over power-line technology, a member of the World Affairs Council of Dallas–Fort Worth, and CEO of Netweavers. She is an executive mentor and coach, an alumna of Leadership Texas, and a frequent speaker at universities and international conferences. Shaunna holds bachelor degrees in mechanical engineering and in education.

**Virginia Gilmore** founded the Sophia Foundation in 2002 to help grow the vision of "creating a more caring community," supporting the spirit, dignity, and potential of every person. After first being introduced to the life and work of Robert Greenleaf in 1996, Ginny has been dedicated to creating teaching and learning communities to support the integration of servant leadership first in her family's manufacturing business, where she spent more than seventeen years in executive leadership, and then at Marian University, where she co-founded the Center for Spirituality and Leadership. Ginny joined with Ann McGee-Cooper and Deborah Welch in 2008 to form and co-facilitate the Virtual Servant Leadership Learning Community (VSLLC®), a program that inspires leaders from around the world.

**Christa Williams** became the first executive director of the Sophia Foundation in 2007. Christa brings her own dedication to the work of Sophia, which is grounded in the belief that every person has strengths to serve and that when we each bring those strengths to the challenges we face in communities, stronger collaborative relationships can be built and address those challenges. Ginny and Christa believe that servant leadership coaching helped build on their individual strengths, gave them the courage to release fears, inspired organizational growth, and helped them overcome obstacles working together at Sophia. Ginny, Christa, and a board of dedicated community servants use the operating principles of servant leadership, dialogue, compassionate listening, and systems thinking to guide the Sophia Foundation. These practices have been translated by the Sophia Foundation into a variety of programs that help the community learn and work together to develop its greatest potential.

**Steve Parker** is director of Sandow Generation, a lignite plant in south central Texas, a part of Luminant Fossil Generation. He has worked for Luminant for thirty-three years. Steve enjoys spending time with family and watching college football.

**Bob Kidwell** was emergency planning manager, Comanche Peak Nuclear Power Plant, where he served for twenty-five years.

**Cliff Watson** is vice president of operations, fossil generation, for Luminant, a competitive power generation subsidiary of Energy Futures Holdings Corp. He is responsible for the safe, reliable, lean, and consistent performance of the three fossil-fueled lignite plants in the Northern Region.

Cliff has worked in a variety of business functions in fossil-fueled lignite and natural gas power generation facilities during his twenty-nine year career with Luminant and its predecessor TXU companies.

Watson earned his bachelor's degree in mechanical engineering from Texas Tech University in 1986. He is a registered professional engineer in Texas. He and his wife have one son and three daughters.

**Madison "Maddie" Watson** is a senior at Dallas Baptist University majoring in communication theory. She enjoys reading, running, and writing. She also enjoys being very involved on campus, as well as in her church. Maddie's family is very special and important to her, so she also loves spending time with them when they all get together. After graduation, Maddie hopes to work in ministry here in the United States or the mission field overseas. She is excited for what is to come, and she knows she will accomplish her dreams through keeping her eyes on the goal ahead.

**Helen Burt** is senior vice president of Corporate Affairs at PG&E Corporation and Pacific Gas and Electric Company. Helen is responsible for leading, aligning and integrating the full spectrum of PG&E's initiatives within federal affairs, state and local government relations, community relations, brand management, advertising, media relations, customer communications, and internal communications. She previously served as chief customer officer and senior vice president of Pacific Gas and Electric Company and was responsible for the overall management of Pacific Gas and Electric Company's customer service organization. She is an experienced customer operations leader with twenty-seven years of experience at TXU (previously known as Texas Utilities).

Helen is a member of the University of California Davis Energy Efficiency Center Board of Advisors, whose mission is to accelerate the development and commercialization of energy efficiency technologies and to train future leaders. She was named one of the 100 Most Influential Women in the Bay Area by the San Francisco Business Times for five consecutive years. In addition, she is a 2004 Fellow of the Broad Foundation Urban Superintendents Academy, with a keen interest and commitment to public education. She spent the ten-month fellowship focusing on improving the nation's largest public school systems.

Helen Burt is a believer and practitioner of servant leadership, integrating these skills into each organization she has served.

# ACKNOWLEDGEMENTS

WE WANT TO DEEPLY THANK EVERYONE who contributed to this book. We especially want to express gratitude to our friends and Partners who have given us such powerful support through your stories, feedback, editing, perspective-giving, caring, and encouragement.

A big thank you to Dawna Markova, Helen Burt, Ginny Gilmore, Christa Williams, Rebecca Braden, Cynthia Watson, Matthew Kosec, Shaunna Black, Jenny Inge, Steve Parker, Cliff Watson, Maddie Watson, Bob Kidwell, Nathan Sowell, Michele Camp, Elena Khoziaeva, Don Frick, Steve Thiry, Michael Sessions, Barbara Dossey, Rick Carson, Kent Keith, Joseph Jaworski, Joel Marquardt, Bill Shira, Allison Bliss, Will Voegele, Thom Welch, Victoria Gamber, Gail Petersen, April Boyington Wall, Midge Miles, Barb Senn, Barb Goodwin, Gail Malay, Mark Arcuri, Carol Haddock, Tara Mibus, Chris Voegele, Luis Fernando Duran-Aparicio, Deborah Costenbader, Timm Chamberlain, and Suzanne Pustejovsky Design.

# ENDNOTES

## Introduction

1. Greenleaf, R. K. (1977). *Servant Leadership: A Journey into the Nature of Legitimate Power and Greatness.* New York, NY: Paulist Press. (p. 7).

2. Some excellent books on servant leadership and business include
   Sisodia, R., Sheth, J. & Wolfe, D. (2014). *Firms of Endearment: How World-Class Companies Profit from Passion and Purpose* (2nd Edition). Upper Saddle River, NJ: Pearson;
   McGee-Cooper, A., Trammell, D., and Kosec, M. (2014). *The Essentials of Servant Leadership: Principles in Practice.* Dallas, TX: AMCA;
   Sipe, J. & Frick, D. (2009) *Seven Pillars of Servant Leadership: Practicing the Wisdom of Leading by Serving.* New York, NY: Paulist Press;
   Keith, K. M. (2008). *The Case for Servant Leadership.* Greenleaf Center for Servant Leadership.

3. Behar, H. (2009). *Leadership Lessons Learned at Starbucks: It's Not About the Coffee.* [DVD]. IMC http://www.insight-media.com/IMC

4. Behar, H. & Goldstein, J. (2009). *It's Not About the Coffee: Lessons on Putting People First from a Life at Starbucks.* Richmond, VA: Portfolio Trade.

## Chapter 1

5. Covey, S. R. (1989). *The 7 Habits of Highly Effective People.* New York, NY: Simon and Schuster.

6. Rath, T., & Conchie, B. (2008). *Strengths-Based Leadership.* New York, NY: Gallup Press.

7. Portions of this interview were first published in Welch, D., Grossaint, K., Reid, K. & Walker, C. (2014). "Strengths-based leadership development: Insights from expert coaches. *Consulting Psychology Journal: Practice and Research, 66,* 20–37. doi: 10.1037/cpb0000002

8. *The Herrmann Brain Dominance Instrument*® HBDI® is available from Herrmann International Lake Lure, NC. Retrieved from http://www.HBDI.com/uploads/100046_Brochures/100678.pdf

9. *The Smart Navigator*® instrument is available from Professional Thinking Partners, Park City, UT. Retrieved from http://ptpinc.org/products-and-services/the-smart-navigator

10. Rath, T., & Conchie, B. (2008). *Strengths-Based Leadership*. New York, NY: Gallup Press.

11. McGee-Cooper, A. & Trammell, D. (1998). *Awakening Your Sleeping Genius: A Journaling Approach to Personal Growth and Servant Leadership*. Dallas, TX: AMCA, Inc. Retrieved from http://amca.com/books-resources/books/awaken-your-sleeping-genius/

12. Greenleaf, R.K. (1979). *Teacher as Servant: A Parable*. New York, NY: Paulist Press.

13. Palmer, P. (2004). *A Hidden Wholeness*. San Francisco, CA: Jossey-Bass.

14. Behar, H. & Goldstein, J. *It's Not About the Coffee*.

15. Sisodia, R., Sheth, J. & Wolfe, D. (2014). *Firms of Endearment: How World-Class Companies Profit from Passion and Purpose* (2nd Edition). Upper Saddle River, NJ: Pearson.

**Chapter 2**

16. Bennis, W. G., & Thomas, R. J. (2002). "Crucibles of Leadership." *Harvard Business Review*, 80(9), 39-45.

17. Jobs, S. (2005). *Commencement Speech*. Speech presented at Stanford University, Stanford Report. Boston, MA. Retrieved from http://news.stanford.edu/news/2005/june15/jobs-061505.html

18. Drake, D. (2012). *Moving from Good to Great: A narrative perspective on strengths*. Presentation at the Positive 2012 Conference in Sydney, Australia, March 12, 2012, pp. 2–25.

19. Senge, P., & Flowers, B. (2009). *Creating New Stories to Shape the Future* (Video Recording). Waltham, MA: Pegasus Communications, Inc.

20. Frankl, V. E. (1985). *Man's Search for Meaning*. Simon and Schuster.

**Chapter 3**

21. Spreitzer, G., Sutcliffe, K., Dutton, J., Sonenshein, S., & Grant, A. M. (2005). "A socially embedded model of thriving at work." *Organization Science*, 16(5), 537-549.

22. Greenleaf, R. K. (2003). *The Servant-Leader Within: A Transformative Path* (p. 19). New Jersey: Paulist Press.

23. Schein, E. H. (2013). *Humble Inquiry: The Gentle Art of Asking Instead of Telling*. San Francisco: Berrett-Koehler Publishers.

24. Covey, S. (1989). *The 7 Habits of Highly Effective People.* New York, NY: Simon and Schuster.

25. Teresa, M. and Kolodiejchuk, B. (2009). *Mother Teresa: Come Be My Light: The Private Writings of the "Saint of Calcutta".* New York, NY: Doubleday.

**Chapter 4**

26. Trammell, D. "Are Your Taillights Flashing?" Retrieved from http://amca.com/amca/wp-content/uploads/Are-Your-Taillights-Flashing-2014.pdf

27. Ibid.

28. McGee-Cooper, A. & Trammell, D. (1998). *Awakening Sleeping Genius: A Journaling Approach to Personal Growth and Servant Leadership.* Dallas, TX: AMCA, Inc. Retrieved from http://amca.com/books-resources/books/awaken-your-sleeping-genius/

29. Greenleaf, R. K., Frick, D., and Spears, L. (1996). Entheos and Growth. In *On Becoming a Servant Leader: The Private Writings of Robert K. Greenleaf.* San Francisco, CA: Jossey-Bass.

30. Greenleaf, R. K. (1977). *Servant Leadership: A Journey into the Nature of Legitimate Power and Greatness.* New York, NY: Paulist Press.

31. Robinson, K. [TED]. (2007, January 6). *Do Schools Kill Creativity?* [Video File] Retrieved from http://www.youtube.com/watch?v=iG9CE55wb+Y.

32. Garland, E. L., Fredrickson, B., Kring, A. M., Johnson, D. P., Meyer, P. S., & Penn, D. L. (2010). "Upward spirals of positive emotions counter downward spirals of negativity: Insights from the broaden-and-build theory and affective neuroscience on the treatment of emotion dysfunctions and deficits in psychopathology." *Clinical Psychology Review, 30*(7), 849-864.

33. Gallwey, T. (1997). *The Inner Game of Tennis: The Classic Guide to the Mental Side of Peak Performance.* New York, NY: Random House.

34. Whyte, D. (2002). *Crossing the Unknown Sea: Work as a Pilgrimage of Identity.* New York, NY: Riverhead Trade.

35. Scharmer, C. O. (2009). *Theory U: Learning from the Future as it Emerges: The Social Technology of Presencing.* San Francisco, CA: Berrett-Koehler Publishers.

36. Jaworski, J. (2012). *Source: The Inner Path of Knowledge Creation.* San Francisco, CA: Berrett-Koehler Publishers.

37. Joel Marquardt's story is not yet published and used with permission.

38. Behar, H. & Goldstein, J. (2009). *It's Not About the Coffee: Lessons on Putting People First from a Life at Starbucks*. Richmond, VA: Portfolio Trade.

39. Brown, J. "Fire." *Teaching with Fire: Poetry that Sustains the Courage to Teach*. Ed. Intrator, S., Scribner, M., Palmer, P. First Edition. San Francisco, CA: Jossey-Bass, 2003.

40. Scharmer, C. O. (2009). *Theory U: Learning from the Future as it Emerges*: *The Social Technology of Presencing*. San Francisco, CA: Berrett-Koehler Publishers.

41. Boelhower, G. (2013). *Choose Wisely: Practical Insights from Spiritual Traditions*. New York, NY: Paulist Press.

**Chapter 5**

42. Two sources that provide more insights on Argyris and the "ladder of inference" are Argyris, C. (1990). *Overcoming Organizational Defenses: Facilitating Organizational Learning*. Upper Saddle River, NJ: Prentice Hall. Senge, P., Kleiner, A., Roberts, C., Ross, R., Smith, B. (1994). *The Fifth Discipline Fieldbook*. New York, NY: Currency, Doubleday.

43. Ellinor, L. & Gerard, G. (1998). *Dialogue: Rediscover the Transforming Power of Conversation*. New York, NY: John Wiley & Sons.

44. Maturana, H & Verden-Zoller, G. (1996). "Biology of Love" in *Focus Heilpadagogik*, ed. Opp, G. & Peterander, F. (Ernst Reinhardt: Munchen/Basel). Retrieved from http://www.lifesnaturalsolutions.com/au/documents/biology-of-love.pdf

**Conclusion**

45. Jaworski, J. (1998). *Destiny and the Leader*. In Spears, *Insights on Leadership: Service, Stewardship, and Servant Leadership*. San Francisco, CA: John Wiley and Sons.

46. Greenleaf, R. K. (1972). *The Institution As Servant*. Indianapolis: Greenleaf Center for Servant Leadership, 1.

47. Wheatley, M. & Frieze, D. (2006). *Using Emergence to Take Social Innovations to Scale*. Retrieved from www.margaretwheatley.com/articles/emergence.htm

48. Palmer, P. (2002). *Personal Communication*, Greenleaf conference.

49. Greenleaf, R. K. (1972). *The Institution as Servant*. Indianapolis, IN: The Robert K. Greenleaf Center.`

# INDEX

accountability, xvi, 105, 121
action plan, 83, 86, 115, 119, 120
active listening, xix, 85, 116, 120
Ann McGee-Cooper & Associates, xii,
  xxi, 124, 126
Appreciation, 82, 93
Argyris, Chris, 90
assuming goodwill, 47–48, 55–56, 116
assumptions, 28, 48, 53, 90–92, 120
*Awakening Your Sleeping Genius: A*
  *Journaling Approach to Personal*
  *Growth and Servant Leadership,* xii, 4,
  63, 124

balance 47, 62, 71, 118
baristas, xvi
Barrett, Colleen, xiv
Behar, Howard, xvi, 12, 73
Bennis, Warren, 22
"Best Companies to Work For", xiv
"Best Test" of servant leadership, xiv, 104
BHAGs, xvi
biographies, 123-129
Black, Shaunna, xxii, 13, 16 127-128,
  131
Blalock, Dr. Alfred, 12
Boelhower, Gary, 78
Braden, Rebecca, xxii, 23, 126, 131
Brown, Judy, 76
Buber, Martin, 27
Burt, Helen, ix-xi, 129, 131

calling, 5-8, 15, 27. 69, 97, 126
caring community, iv, 75, 128
celebration, 82, 93-94, 115
change, iv, v, x, xii, xx, 9, 12, 15, 20,
  23, 27-28, 44-45, 62, 67, 71, 73-74,
  76, 87-88, 96, 109, 115-119, 123-
  124, 126
coach, iii, x-xi, xv, xviii, xix-xx, xxii,
  1, 2, 4, 6, 9, 11-12, 14-15, 17, 23,
  33, 36, 38, 41-42, 44-46, 48-49, 52-
  53, 57, 64, 71, 74, 76-77, 79, 81,
  83, 86, 88-89, 94, 96-97, 99, 101,
  104-105, 108-109, 116, 118-119, 121,
  126, 128

coachability, 82
coaching, iv, x-xiii, xv-xvi, xviii, xix-
  xxiii, 2-5, 9, 10, 13-17, 19-20, 23,
  25-29, 34-36, 38-39, 41-44, 46, 49-
  52, 54-55, 57-58, 60, 67-68, 71-79,
  81-88, 94-96, 99, 101, 104, 106,
  108-109, 111-112, 115-117, 119, 124,
  126, 128
coaching notes, xxiii, 115
coaching relationships, xv, 101
"Coaching with a Servant's Heart", xvi,
  4, 17, 36, 44, 58, 79, 108-109
collaboration, 40, 96, 124
collaborative intelligence, xii, 30, 33, 69,
  124-125
communities, iv, xv, 125, 128
community, iv, xii, xix, xx-xii, 52, 61,
  64-65, 74-75, 77-78, 96, 123-126,
  128
conflict, xvi, 32, 42, 92
continuous improvement, 13
contributors, xxii, xxiii, 39, 123, 125
conversation, xix, 10, 12, 23, 27-29, 51,
  66, 76-77, 90, 92, 109
Covey, Stephen, 1, 55
*Crossing the Unknown Sea,* 70
culture, xii, xiv, xv, xviii, xxi, 13-16,
  33-34, 40, 90, 123, 126
cynicism, xxi, 67

Dallas, i, ii, xii, xxi, 8, 101, 124-125,
  127-129
decision fatigue, 46
dialogue, 14, 27, 33, 55, 57, 74, 84,
  92, 95, 100, 112, 117, 128
*Dialogue: Rediscover the Transforming*
  *Power of Conversation,* 92
discovery, xvi, 19, 49, 96-97, 100, 104
diversity, 40
doctoral students, xxi
Drake, David, 26

ego, iv, 9, 23, 44, 56, 73, 95,
Einstein, Albert, 76, 119
Ellinor, Linda, 92
empathy, 6, 8, 20, 23, 25, 33, 54, 109

McGee-Cooper, Ann, ix-xii, xviii-xxiii,
    4-7, 9-10, 14, 21, 26, 28, 30, 42,
    46-52, 58, 62-68, 72, 83-89, 93-96,
    101, 111, 118, 123-124, 128
Mead, Dr. Margaret, 123
mental models, 29, 90
mentor, 22, 23, 44, 48, 65, 66, 97, 104
metaphors, 53
mirroring, xix, 35, 93, 116
mirrors, 53-54, 56
mission, xvi, xviii, 8, 78
Montessori, 7
Mother Teresa, 56

neural hijacking, 67-68

open-ended questions, 52
organizational challenges, xv
organizational chart, xx
organizational takeover, xxi
ownership, 36, 82-83, 85, 94, 121-122

Palmer, Parker, 10-12, 105
Parker, Steve, xxii, 100, 111-113, 128,
    131
partner, x, xii, xiv, xx, 3-4, 12, 14, 30,
    35, 41, 46-48, 57, 62, 67, 74-76, 79,
    83, 95, 104-105, 109
partnering iv, 13, 30, 38, 42, 74, 75
partners, 2, 5, 9, 10, 12-13, 20, 26-27,
    38, 41, 52, 54, 66-69, 73-74, 76,
    100-101, 104-105
partnership, iv, xii, 13, 32, 38, 42, 53,
    58, 61, 74-75, 78, 96, 104
passion, xvii-xviii, 12, 16, 106, 125,
    126
peer, xx, 12, 52, 121
performance, ix, xiv, xv, 13, 15, 28,
    32, 69, 84, 87, 106, 112, 129
personal calling, 5
PG&E Corporation, xi
place of belonging, 71
plus/delta, 82, 89, 95, 109, 116
potential, ix-xi, xviii,, 4, 13, 16-17, 29,
    41, 51, 61, 63-64, 68-69, 72, 75, 78,
    89, 96, 109, 112, 128
practices, xvi, xix, xxiii, 15, 49, 70-72,
    77-78, 82, 89, 93, 99, 108, 116, 128

principles, xiii, xv, xx-xxiii, 10, 36, 53,
    100, 104, 106, 113, 123, 128
professional coaches, xx, xxii
purpose, xxii, 2, 9, 11, 16, 27, 34, 41,
    52, 58, 64, 70, 72, 104, 106, 112,
    119, 125

reciprocity, 29
Reflections, xvi, 17, 36, 43, 58, 79, 96
relational intelligence, 69
relationship, iv, v, xiv, xv, 3, 21, 28-
    29, 30, 34, 38-39, 41-42, 48, 52-53,
    56, 74, 76, 86, 101, 109
relationships, xv, xvi, xx, 37-38, 42,
    46, 48, 52-54, 56-58, 60, 74, 90,
    101, 104, 126-128
respect, xiv, 6, 27, 40, 44, 47, 57-58,
    79, 82, 85-86, 95-96, 113, 116, 118
reverence, xix
Rilke, Rainer, 71
Robinson, Sir Ken, 65
role model, 63, 83, 119

sarcasm, 87
Scharmer, Otto, 72, 77, 105
Schein, Edgar, 52
Schultz, Howard, xvi
self-awareness, v, xi-xii, 9, 28, 44, 55-
    56, 60, 86, 105, 108, 118, 124
self-discovery, x, 95, 100, 108
self-esteem, 87
self-fulfilling prophecy, 87
self-growth, 56-57
self-knowledge, 14
self-managing teams, xxi
self-talk, 28
Senge, Peter, 26
servant-leader, x-xvi, xviii, xx-xxi, 1-2,
    4-6, 9-12, 14, 16-17, 20, 23-24, 46,
    48, 52, 55, 57, 62-64, 66, 71, 73,
    76-77, 81, 83, 95, 97, 99, 100-101,
    104-105, 111, 117, 122, 124
servant leadership, iv, x, xii-xxiii, 2, 4,
    8, 13-15, 17, 19-21, 25, 27, 30, 33,
    35, 42, 46-47, 52-54, 57, 61, 63-66,
    68, 73-75, 78, 81, 83, 85-86, 97, 99-
    101, 103-104, 106, 108-109, 113,
    115, 123, 126, 128, 129

Made in the USA
Middletown, DE
16 November 2015